Powered Up

PoWERED UP

Turning your strengths into superpowers

NiCOLE WEBER

Published by Nicole Weber

First published in 2024 in Jindabyne, Australia

Copyright© Nicole Weber

www.nicoleweber.com.au

Graphics created by Nicole Weber

Edited by Jenny Magee

Typeset and printed in Australia by BookPOD

ISBN: 978-1-7637700-0-3 (paperback)
ISBN: 978-1-7637700-1-0 (ebook)

A catalogue record for this book is available from the National Library of Australia

Within each of us there is the heart of a lion, the courage to simply be who and what we are regardless of others' opinions or our own fears. Sometimes this courage has been buried beneath years of shaming that may have been so implicit or insidious that we breathed it in, unaware of how it separated us from knowing our own beauty of being. May we each know our own beauty and right to be today. May we drop down into the heart of the lion within and say to shame, when it rears its head, "Not today!"

– Oriah Dreamer

ACKNOWLEDGEMENTS

I acknowledge the Ngarigo and Dharawal people, the Traditional Custodians of the land where I live and where I wrote much of this book. I recognise their continuing connection to land, water and community, and I am grateful for the care First Nations people across Australia have given to the country over many millennia.

Thank you to Kieren, Ryan, Ash, Mum & Dad, Angela & John. For different reasons, you are all my superheroes.

Thank you to Jenny Magee, editor and author coach extraordinaire. I could not have brought this book into the world without your wisdom and guidance.

Massive gratitude to the following fine people interviewed for this, my first book. They have enabled me to be a better coach and consultant. You are listed in reverse alphabetical order because we Ws are always at the back of the line.

Sandra Wood
Kate Webber
Peggy Webb
Mary Rezek
Tanya Murray-Russell
Donna Osmetti
Christopher Miller

Steve Klaassen
Kerry Grace
Tracy Duncan
Nicole Black

CLIFTONSTRENGTHS® ACKNOWLEDGEMENT

CONTENTS

PART ONE

INTRODUCTION

Have you ever played that game where you debated which superpower you would rather have? If so, chances are you picked something like x-ray vision or invisibility. If you're old-school, you might have gone for physical strength, super speed (hello, Wonder Woman) or the ability to leap tall buildings in a single bound (good old Superman). Possessing superpowers suggests we have superhuman strengths. We are talented, confident and capable of amazing feats.

But I'm here to confirm that you do indeed have superpowers. You just don't necessarily know them yet. (Stay with me on this one.)

For many of us, though, self-doubt lurks in the shadows, a warning light on our self-esteem dashboard that appears when we're under pressure. For some people, self-doubt is ever-present; a flashing neon sign above their heads, yelling *'Imposter'*. Fearing that you might be exposed as a fraud is the very opposite of a superhero.

Feeling that you are not enough or not giving your best is a surefire way to deplete your energy and sap your confidence. It may surface at certain times in your life or hum below the surface for years or even decades. It is common for people to experience feelings of low confidence or self-worth.

In the late 1990s, a group of psychologists became interested in studying what might boost human wellbeing in a move away from the traditional psychology focus on mental ill-health. Martin Seligman and Mihaly Csikszentmihalyi (pronounced *Cheek-sent-me-hi*) were leaders in this field of positive psychology.[1] In his book *Authentic Happiness,* Seligman's key message is that if you want greater happiness, you must know your strengths and use them every day in key areas of your life.[2]

Research by Csikszentmihalyi shows that when you can name and use your strengths, you are much happier, feel more energised, and find a state of flow.[3] Our strengths are a big part of what makes us who we are.

People who know their strengths and can put into words when and how they use them (and even misuse them) have a significant advantage.

Our strengths are our *superpowers*.

What about you? Can you name your strengths? Can you describe what they look like in action? Do you recognise when they get in your way or show up as weaknesses?

From an early age, we are taught to focus on fixing our weaknesses, yet building on our strengths is far more effective. When we pay attention to our strengths, particularly during times of stress, we can create an emotional buffer and sense of optimism. The great news is that this buffer is active during the stressful period and beyond.[4]

I am fascinated by the strengths that make people unique. Those qualities that make you, *you*. I wrote this book because I want more people to know themselves better through the lens of strengths and tap into their superpowers. As a coach, manager, parent and friend, I have seen the incredible impact of strengths across all areas of life.

I am a better coach because I know and use my strengths. I help others find and use their strengths (aka personal superpowers) to transform their results at work and their relationships. I want everyone to know what it is like to know their strengths and use them as personal superpowers. I call this Powering Up.

How to use this book

I am highly practical and believe that the power of strengths is in their application. In this book, I've drawn together tried and tested tools and strategies to build self-awareness, self-management and self-mastery. All by applying your strengths thoughtfully and deliberately.

While we can never really coach ourselves (we are way too close to the action to be objective), my aim in this book is to get you thinking with a coaching mindset. I want to set you on the road to self-mastery. In my coaching, I encourage clients to complete the CliftonStrengths® assessment so they have a validated and trustworthy strengths profile. The assessment is an excellent investment that will cost you about the same as four cocktails, minus the boozy hangover. The insights and opportunities revealed are worth every cent.

There are various strengths tools available, which we'll explore in the section titled Discovering Strengths. Any strengths report will give you interesting information. You will gain new insights and have some 'Aha' moments, but shifting from interesting to transformative needs a pathway. This book will take you on that journey.

I have written this book in two parts. Part One introduces you to the three elements of my Powered Up Strengths model: **self-awareness** is understanding how strengths show up, **self-management** is knowing how to use them skilfully, and **self-mastery** means applying the right strength at the right time with the right intensity. These are the building blocks for taking you from strengths discovery to skilful application and collaboration with others. Part Two describes how to apply your Powered Up strengths to three key areas of life: work, connecting and relating to others and thriving in the face of challenges.

Each chapter includes real-life examples, quotes and some go-to coaching questions to keep in your back pocket. I have designed each section for you to apply to your life. Please make time to pause, reflect and make notes as you go. Doing so will deepen your knowledge of the ideas and of yourself.

This book was not designed to be read through in one sitting and then filed on your shelf (or regifted or left on a bus or the lunchroom table for someone else to take home).

I recommend reading this introductory session and following the process outlined. Discover your strengths and practice the Powered Up approach to self-awareness right through to self-mastery. Then, consider how strengths show up in the different areas of your life, such as those outlined in Part Two.

Strengths need practice to reach their potential. By practising each step along the way, you will build your strengths in unique ways that work best for your life. In this way, the book is more than interesting reading; it is a guide to putting your strengths to work and Powering them Up!

What exactly are strengths?

Given all the personality tests and diagnostic tools so widely promoted, strengths might seem like another buzzword or fad. You may be confused or unclear about what strengths really are. The practice of positive psychology (the optimal functioning of people) has been around for more than 40 years. Character strengths are 'positive and enduring personal characteristics expressed through thoughts, feelings and behaviour that help a person to flourish'.[5]

Another definition of strengths is 'the natural abilities you are motivated to use, combining your character, experience and skills being applied to an activity which makes you feel your true self and at your best'.[6]

In plain language, I describe strengths as 'how you show up in the world'. They are a filter or lens for your thoughts and show up in your behaviour. You feel energised, engaged and motivated when you use your strengths to their best potential. They help you to flourish and succeed in life. When you are in situations that don't allow you to use your strengths, or you misuse or overuse them, you are likely to feel frustrated and uninspired.

What's the science behind strengths?

When it comes to strengths, the original superheroes were those who pioneered positive psychology. Donald Clifton started thinking and writing about the science of strengths around 1949.[7] As an academic at Nebraska University, he noticed that successful students had noticeably different character traits from those who were less successful. His research found that success had more to do with character and traits (such as perseverance) than smarts.

In the 1970s, Alice Isen and her colleagues looked at the links between positive emotions and cognitive outcomes.[8] Their research ranged from testing people doing cognitive puzzles to simulations of life-and-death situations. In a series of studies over many years, these psychologists found that positive emotions boosted cognitive flexibility, intrinsic motivation, receptivity to new information, and improved problem-solving.[9,10,11]

Mihaly Csikszentmihalyi built on these ideas with the concept of flow, in which a person is fully interested and engaged in a task that is sufficiently challenging and matched to their strengths.[12] At the end of the 1990s, Csikszentmihalyi and Seligman collaborated to set up the field of positive psychology. Their goal was an increased focus on the study of positive human functioning and understanding what makes a 'good life'.[13]

Around this time, Donald Clifton worked with a team of psychologists to develop the CliftonStrengths® tool. First released as a book and later online, it outlines 34 different strengths aligned with four themes: executing, influencing, relationship building and strategic thinking.[14]

In 2004, Christopher Peterson and Martin Seligman created the Values in Action Inventory of Strengths, known as the VIA Character Strengths assessment tool and handbook.[15] This tool identifies six universal virtues and 24 character strengths. As with CliftonStrengths®, it is highly regarded and well-utilised.

In the section on Discovering Strengths, I'll introduce you to some tools you can use to uncover your strengths. The frameworks I refer to are all created by psychologists and tested for their reliability. You can confidently apply them, knowing they are verified through a scientific process.

At the time of writing this book, the counter on the Gallup® website showed that the CliftonStrengths® tool had been taken more than 32 million times worldwide since its first release. While that number does not account for people exploring their strengths using other tools, it does show people's enduring and global interest in understanding who they are at their best.

Imagine what would happen if every workplace had a strengths-based culture. How different might workplaces look and feel? Positive psychology research shows that people who know and use their strengths at work are half as stressed, twice as engaged and almost 8% more productive than those who do not know and use their strengths.[16] Amplify that power across Australia's more than 2.5 million workplaces and consider what could be achieved.

Let's think local. What if *your* workplace, family, or community group had a strengths culture? Imagine what that would look and feel like. What challenges or issues could you tackle more easily or differently if everyone around you knew and used their strengths?

Why do strengths matter?

Have you ever wondered what your 'one of a kind' contribution to the world is?

Sandra Wood has coached thousands of people across her career. She has worked as a human resources practitioner and managed teams. For over 20 years Sandra has run her own business as a leadership consultant, and she has spent much of that time delivering Great Managers®, a powerful and practical management training program she developed. Across all her work, Sandra has questioned, challenged and nudged people toward better self-awareness. As Sandra describes it, strengths are the unique blueprint of your contribution. She says:

'It's conditioned into us at a very early age. It's hardwired into the way our primitive brain works and part of the way the ego works. The ego is all about protecting us, keeping us safe, but also keeping us playing small. It's that feeling that "I'm not enough. I'm not enough as I am".

'When people learn that they've got this set of strengths, it can help to override that feeling. Everyone wants to feel enough, like they're adding value and contributing, and have meaning and purpose in their lives. And yet that feeling of "I'm not enough how I am" undermines their life experience. You have a unique blueprint of strengths that the world needs. And if you can activate that and operate from that, that's your contribution.'

Life can be hard and overwhelming. Navigating work, relationships, friendships and life's general ups and downs takes energy and effort. When your default mindset is 'I am not enough', it sucks your energy. Feeling like you are not bringing your best is the opposite of an inspired life.

Think of your strengths as a renewable energy source – like the sun on a solar panel – powering enthusiasm, connection and commitment. That is what you experience when you are in flow and working in your strengths zone. The more you can use your strengths, the more energised you will become.

That energy converts to results. Better connections to others through improved relationships. Better outcomes through more focus and commitment that make the most of your one-of-a-kind contribution.

Are we ignoring weaknesses?

Even superheroes have weaknesses. Batman's arrogance and overconfidence are used against him. Wonder Woman gets entangled in her Lasso of Truth. Superman's vulnerability to kryptonite, a substance that takes away his strength, is well known.

When you hear the word 'strengths', you might automatically add 'and weaknesses'. We are socially conditioned to see strengths as something to celebrate and weaknesses as personal failures. We are often told to fix our weaknesses before focusing on our strengths. Yet, perhaps surprisingly, weaknesses are usually the result of overusing or misusing a strength. I'll talk more about this in the next chapter.

For now, I want to add some context. Imagine the extreme effort and concentration it would take to meditate at a rock concert.

Now compare that with meditating next to a bubbling stream or in the peace of a yoga studio. When we focus on fixing our weaknesses, it's like meditating at a rock concert. The effort versus reward is minimal. Understanding and applying our strengths to their full potential requires much less effort, and we get the most out of our energy. We are working on something we are already naturally good at.

Knowing and skillfully using our strengths allows us to be experts at spotting and wrangling our weaknesses. We can better see and manage weaknesses by using strengths as the viewfinder. You see, weaknesses are the flip side – the shadow side – of strengths.

Alex was one of my first clients when I trained as a strengths coach. When we met, things were not going well for Alex. If you were a fly-on-the-wall observer, you might say she had many weaknesses that were causing havoc in her life.

At work, Alex clashed with her colleagues and her manager. She was a case worker in Juvenile Justice and described herself as burnt out, sad, and worn out. Alex had been taken off frontline work after sending confrontational emails to her manager. She was now assigned administrative duties for three months and was being counselled about her actions.

At home, Alex was faring worse. She and her partner had recently separated and were struggling to co-parent their three young children. Alex said that despite best efforts on both sides, each time the children came to her new home, she and her ex-partner would argue about some details of the children's care. Alex felt stuck in a negative communication pattern she didn't know how to break out of.

Alex's strengths include empathy and communication, which might surprise you when you read her story. One of the remarkable aspects of strengths is that they can show up as weaknesses. Recognising this can unlock new understanding of behaviour.

After several coaching sessions, Alex saw that her work in juvenile justice required a lot of empathy. She had been taking on the emotional load of her clients, their families and colleagues, but had not put any strategies in place to protect her emotional wellbeing.

She could also see she was overusing her communication strength rather than using it skilfully. The combative emails to her manager were an example. Alex realised that when she argued with her ex-partner, she bombarded him with information and expected him to reply on the spot. Armed with better self-awareness, Alex suggested that they use a notebook to share information about their children and include any non-urgent questions in it. The notebook acted as a circuit-breaker for the pattern they had both fallen into and proved successful.

When Alex was in the thick of the situation, her strengths ran riot and hindered positive results across different areas of her life. She was too close to the action to see what was happening. Everything felt messy and out of control. As we worked together,

Alex looked at her weaknesses through a strengths lens and took practical steps that played to those strengths.

Digging into our strengths does not mean we are ignoring weaknesses. Far from it. We understand them differently, allowing us to see how overplayed or misused strengths can show up or get in our way. Knowing this, we can avoid and manage our weaknesses. It is a critical part of the Powered Up process.

If you still need convincing, consider the following ten reasons to know and use your strengths.

Why listen to me?

I have worked within a strengths-based framework since my career began over 25 years ago. I first learned how the strengths approach was used in communities and families to create positive change. As a naturally positive person, it made sense to me that change was more likely to happen when we focussed on what people could *do* rather than what they could *not*. Like a kid discovering soft drinks, I was hooked on this approach and fizzed with the possibilities. Right away, I started using my strengths as a manager, working in community development and helping workplaces thrive.

In 2016, I became a Gallup® certified strengths coach. When I took the CliftonStrengths® assessment, read my report and trained as an accredited coach, it was like having a zing moment. I finally felt seen, understood and energised by the power and possibilities of my strengths. Better yet, I had found a framework and language to connect with and use to help others build their confidence and skills. It fired up a fierce energy in me that I feel even now.

Throughout my career, I have used the strengths approach with thousands of people in team and individual coaching and development programs. I still get a huge thrill when I see others click when they tap into the power of their strengths.

In this book, I want to ignite that powerful zing in you and thousands of other readers. I want you to feel the confidence, clarity and personal power that knowing and skilfully using your strengths can bring.

Strengths rock!

Don't just take my word for it. One of the best ways to understand strengths is to hear reflections from other people – not celebrities or gurus, but everyday people: family, friends, colleagues and others.

When I decided to write this book, I wanted to know what others thought of strengths: their own and those around them. So, I approached people in my network who have deliberately and thoughtfully tapped into strengths. Throughout this book, you will find stories and practical examples from my experiences and a bunch of generous and knowledgeable folks. I've interviewed coaches, leaders and some of my coaching clients to get their take on strengths. I hope their insights resonate with you as well. Their words are far more potent than sharing headline quotes from experts or crusty old dudes who are long dead.

The stories I share are from real coaching scenarios. I have changed some names and details for confidentiality reasons. These stories illustrate the power of strengths in ways that you will connect with. When I interviewed people for this book, I asked, 'What did you get from discovering your strengths?' There were clear themes; here is a snapshot of what they told me.

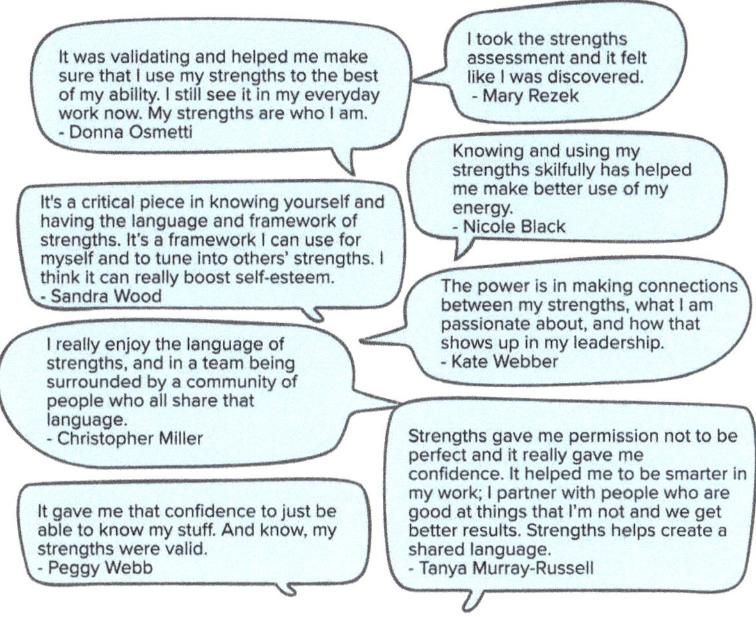

Surf the strengths wave

Using your strengths can boost confidence, offer a sense of authenticity and give a significant charge of energy. You may have experienced this without realising you had jumped onboard one of your strengths and were surfing it like the perfect wave.

> 'A strength comes easily to us; it's almost autonomic and feels natural. That's where the energy comes from. When you're using a strength, not much effort is required.'
>
> – Sandra Wood.

When you catch a wave in the ocean, there is a sense of enormous energy as the wave builds momentum and carries you along. You are swept up and propelled forward. Waves are a perpetual and powerful energy source, and you can view strengths in the same way. Strengths hold their energy.

Here's what happens when you ride the WAVE of your strengths.

When you're immersed in an activity and notice some or all these factors, take a moment to consider what strengths are being leveraged. Combining the four dimensions of the strengths, WAVE allows you to apply this powerful source of energy, momentum and enthusiasm to everyday challenges.

We sometimes experience waves of challenging emotions such as fear, fatigue and frustration. These are also worth noticing as they present an opportunity to think about how to catch a strengths WAVE instead. How could you apply your strengths to the challenge to shift your emotions and the outcome?

Set your intention

Before you go any further, I want you to think clearly about what you want to change, because creating change takes work. When you set an intention, you prime your brain for change. Without this priming, you will spin in circles, using a lot of energy and going nowhere fast. Setting an intention is like putting on your superhero costume. You are preparing for action. So, picture your costume now. You might even like to sketch it out.

When setting your intention for what you want to change and the results you are looking for, ask yourself the following coaching questions. Remember what I said earlier, and make time to think fully about your answers. Writing them down will inspire greater insight.

Your Back Pocket Coach

Hand on heart, what is one strength you know you have? Name three things this strength has helped you achieve?

What one thing are you prepared to do more of, to know and use your strengths every day?

What is one thing you may need to do less of, to know and use your strengths every day?

What weakness do you feel you need to fix? If this weakness was in fact, an overused strength, which strength would it be?

On the following scale, rate how often you think about your weaknesses.

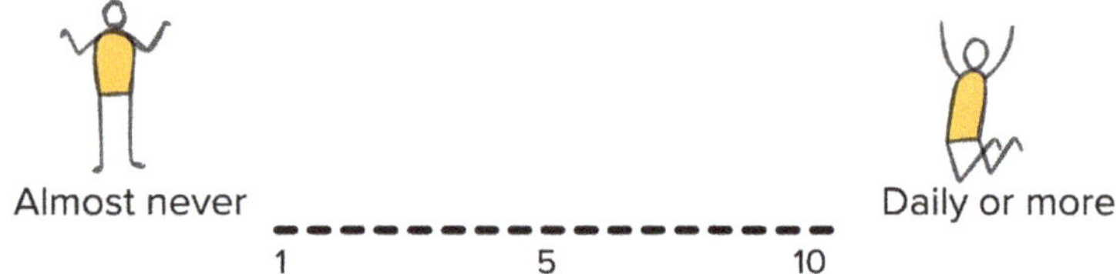

Now use the same scale and rate how often you think about your strengths. Is it more or less often than weaknesses? Make an effort to switch from thinking about weaknesses to noticing strengths.

TIME TO GET POWERED UP

To show up as your best self, you must fully understand *why* you think, feel and behave as you do. That's *self-awareness*. Then, you can use that understanding to make shifts and changes and create new habits that will get better results. That's *self-management*. When you can do both of these, you can better control your superpowers and move your focus to influencing and collaborating in skilful and thoughtful ways. That's *self-mastery*.

Strengths are often an untapped or underappreciated resource. When used skilfully and deliberately, they have enormous potential. When we take the information from a strengths assessment and apply our strengths masterfully, we power up our strengths. We allow our strengths to work to their full and unique potential.

Like any skilful practice, achieving self-mastery requires a sustained and deliberate effort. Building muscle strength takes time and repeatedly lifting heavy weights. Building character strength requires a commitment to habits of self-awareness and self-management. It means overriding our deeply entrenched urges and habits.

We need to notice and be curious when we feel energised and 'in the zone' to see how our strengths work well for us. We also need to pull ourselves up when things are not going well, when we feel frustrated, or when we are getting in our own way. If you have heard the saying, 'butting your head against a brick wall', that is what it looks like when we do the same awkward thing over and over and expect a different result. It is a great description of a lack of self-awareness and self-management.

I have thought long and hard about what it takes to get from frustration to that 'Yes!' triumphant air-punch moment. I saw a clear, three-stage process that became the Powered Up model.

The Powered Up process

There are three steps to knowing and using your strengths to their full potential:

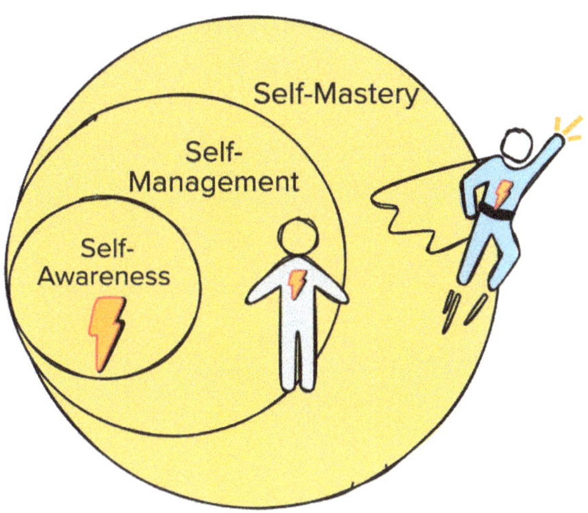

Self-Awareness: Here, we name our strengths and describe them in action, both when they work for us and when they get in our way. When we put effort into awareness, we sharpen those tools and work out how to use our strengths best. This step prepares us for the next.

Self-Management: We thoughtfully respond to situations using the right strength at the right time. In this stage, we better appreciate our strengths and are more forgiving of our failings, allowing us to adopt a growth or a learner mindset. When we do this, we maximise our energy. Instead of giving ourselves a hard time, we recognise when our strengths are overused or misused. Then, we identify a better approach by using our strengths differently and moving on. There is much potential here to improve self-confidence.

Self-Mastery: This means applying the right strength at the right time, with the right intensity. We are curious and aware of others' strengths and can achieve remarkable results by partnering our strengths with theirs. Relationships transform because our mindset is different and we move more readily from judgement to empathy.

You will notice that each step builds on those before it. As we move through them, we continue to develop the insights and tools that help us power up our strengths.

This book steps through each stage with practical tools to reach self-mastery.

Your Back Pocket Coach

When did you most recently use one of your strengths?
What did this strength help you do? How did you use it?

Which strength do you admire most in others?
What does that strength help them get done?
What does that strength look like in action?
Which of your strengths could you use to get a similar result?

What three words would the people who know you best use to describe you?
How does it feel when you use a strength?
What changes do you notice in your energy?

POWERING UP SELF-AWARENESS

Self-awareness is your first power skill

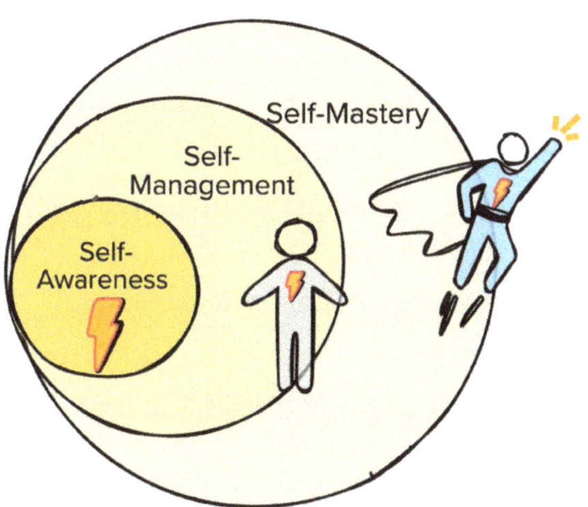

Imagine a mini version of yourself perched on your shoulder, whispering real-time feedback in your ear like a helpful sports commentator. It might sound like this: 'Hmm, Nicole, you are reacting strongly to what that person just said. Is that a bit of frustration bubbling up? Be careful; it's showing on your face. You are starting to shut down a bit. You need to ask a question before you jump to conclusions.'

Self-awareness is the ability to notice our thoughts, feelings and behaviour in real-time. It allows us to step back and see ourselves objectively. Of course, this is much easier said than done. Like many life skills, it is learned.

I began my career as a caseworker gifted with a fantastic supervisor. Sue was the senior social worker at the health service where I worked. From the start, I met with Sue each month for clinical supervision. She taught me invaluable self-reflection skills. Initially, our conversations were brutally honest and uncomfortable. (For me, at least; I think she secretly enjoyed watching me squirm and grow.)

At that early point in my career, I had not set up the habits of reflection and critical thinking crucial to working in social welfare without burning out. Completing a social welfare degree gave me many theories about human behaviour, social systems and dominant ideologies of the time. However, I needed a deep working knowledge of how to get out of my own way and work skilfully with an endless stream of clients trying to navigate a complex social service system.

I worked with older people who needed support to stay at home or higher-level care in a residential setting. I worked with families in crisis, older people who were experiencing neglect or abuse, and people who quite cheerfully told me that they 'had had a great life and were now disappointed that they woke up each morning'.

As the welfare officer, I was seen as the general dogsbody in a team of nurses and doctors. I was often assigned clients who needed help filling in forms or other tasks considered too mundane for the health professionals I worked with. There was a wide range of functions and it took a great deal of energy to manage the client work and the team dynamics.

Early in this role, I bounced from one situation to the next, doing my best to respond to whatever was in front of me. I brought my values and beliefs and the strong work ethic my parents instilled in me. I worked hard – but I could have been wiser. I was like a pinball in a machine, rocketing from one task and interaction to the next, draining my energy as I went.

Clinical supervision with Sue helped me unpack the most challenging of these situations. Sue taught me how to step back and consider my work in a much more objective way. Her questions got me thinking critically about how my values and strengths showed up in my work. I learned to 'do with', not 'do to' when working with clients. Recognising the difference and how I could work with my skills and strengths more intentionally became the foundation of my practice. I still draw on this groundwork, which has been a consistent thread throughout my career. Thank you, Sue!

Discovering strengths

Self-awareness starts with knowing your strengths. A word of warning, though: learning about your strengths will open an entire world of self-discovery, and it won't all be a barrel of laughs. You may discover some uncomfortable truths. The wonderful thing about self-awareness is that you will add skills to navigate everyday joys and trials. If you think of life as a journey at sea, self-awareness gives you a rudder to steer yourself rather than bobbing along carried by winds and currents.

> 'Learning about your strengths is like upgrading your operating system. A system upgrade doesn't mean you have to change who you are. It doesn't mean there's anything wrong with you. It's just that you have new awareness and understanding. I ask my clients, "What do you want to do with this information?" It's about knowing what your strengths are telling you about yourself. What energises you, and what do you love? And how can you take care of yourself through your strengths?'
>
> – Mary Rezek.

There are several ways to learn what your strengths are. In his book, *Go Put Your Strengths to Work*, Marcus Buckingham suggests that we can capably self-identify our strengths.[1] From my personal experience of discovering my strengths and coaching others to uncover theirs, I respectfully disagree. We are simply too close to the action to fully appreciate our strengths. We might imagine we have strengths that aren't there, or miss some of our strengths because we don't give ourselves credit for them.

I'll give you an example. I have always thought of myself as a highly empathetic person. When I read my CliftonStrengths® report, I discovered that my empathy comes from a combination of several different strengths. I now appreciate all these strengths and how they work together. I would not have known this without doing a strengths assessment.

However, if you are looking for a starting point, I have included a list of strengths at the back of this book. Review the list and choose 8-10 that you think are yours.

You might ask other people to tell you what they think your strengths are. Choose 3-5 people who know you well. Send them the following through email or text and see what comes back.

Hi (name), I am doing some self-development work, and I am keen to know what you think my strengths are. I would appreciate you letting me know.

The best (and the most accurate) way to identify your strengths is to complete an online strengths assessment tool. There are several available, and they will each give slightly different information. To be upfront, I am a certified CliftonStrengths® coach, so that is my preferred tool. The following online strengths tools were developed by psychologists. Check them out and compare them for yourself.

CliftonStrengths® was developed by Don Clifton and Marcus Buckingham. The tool allows you to explore 34 strengths, organised into four key themes or domains. I find this tool helps people understand and apply strengths across all areas of life and is the most individualised and versatile of the strengths tools I have used. You can find it at https://www.gallup.com/cliftonstrengths/en/252137/home.aspx

The **VIA Character Strengths** tool was developed by Christopher Peterson and Martin Seligman and outlines 24 character strengths or virtues across six domains. As this tool is free, it offers a low-risk option for exploring strengths. In my experience, this tool can spark great strengths conversations at home and in some workplaces. Some strengths, such as humour, love and forgiveness, can be challenging to apply in many workplaces. You can find this tool at https://www.viacharacter.org

A third tool is **Stand Out** created by Marcus Buckingham, which outlines nine strengths roles. As this is another free assessment, it can provide a different perspective on your strengths without cost. In my experience, this tool offers a fairly generic strengths profile rather than the deeply individualised insights found in CliftonStrengths®. If you are keen on another strengths perspective, you can find Stand Out here: https://www.tmbc.com/.

There are other strengths tools out there that I haven't covered here. Whichever you choose, one of the greatest benefits is that it provides language to talk about your strengths. Even better, if others in your workplace, family, or other social circles also take a strengths assessment, you will have a common language to describe how you process information and behave. It opens a whole new world of communication.

> 'What CliftonStrengths® does very well is that it gives you a much longer list of strengths than you thought were available. Your vocabulary increases and describes the strengths that you have.'
>
> – Steve Klaassen.

I was surprised when I first read my CliftonStrengths® profile. On reflection, this was because my strengths are so much part of who I am that I did not consider them strengths until they were spelled out in my report. I mean, doesn't everyone have a plan and a backup plan for the next six or twelve months, five and ten years? Apparently not. Some people think planning is a foreign (and even repugnant) concept. Yet planning is an example of my Futuristic® and Strategic® strengths in action. They influence so much of what I do, but I was too close to them – I couldn't see the wood for the trees..

> 'It's a critical part of knowing yourself, which many people struggle with. They say, "I can tell you my weakness, but a strength?" It's like they can feel that sense of the unknown.'
>
> – Sandra Wood.

The experience Sandra refers to is common, as we are socialised to focus on our weaknesses. Some of us have been actively discouraged from naming or exploring our strengths. To do so might have been labelled as big-noting or being 'up yourself'. Yet the CliftonStrengths® tool alone has been taken more than 32 million times. That many people cannot be wrong. Our strengths matter to us, and they should matter to others.

FAQs about strengths finding

Before you take any strengths assessment, here are some Frequently Asked Questions to help you get the most out of these tools.

Q: How long will the assessment take?

A: This varies between assessments; however, CliftonStrengths® and the VIA Character Strengths Survey take up to 45 minutes to complete.

Q: Does it matter when I do the assessment?

A: You will get the most accurate results if you complete a strengths assessment when you feel emotionally 'even', not highly stressed, emotional or in a rush.

Q: How much thought should I put into my answers?

A: Go with your gut feeling. When you take the assessments I mentioned, you will be shown two words or statements and asked which is 'most like you'. To get the most accurate results, answer honestly and without overthinking. Respond according to how you are now, not how you want to be in the future. Some assessments give a limited time to answer to discourage overthinking. I also recommend that you don't choose the neutral option. The tool can't read your mind; it needs enough data to give you an accurate report.

Q: Do our strengths stay the same as we age, or do they change?

A: The consensus is that our strengths stay relatively stable from around age 17. If you took the same strengths assessment every decade, your strengths profile would likely be similar each time. The order of the strengths in your report might shuffle a little, but your dominant strengths (your top 10) would be more or less the same.

Q: Is the order of my strengths on the report significant?

A: I encourage people to think about their strengths (particularly their top 5 or 10) as a toolbox. We draw on different strengths at different times and may lean more heavily on some than others. Rather than getting too hung up on the order of your strengths, see them as a collective.

Q: What do I do with my report when I get it?

A: Print out your report and read it. Highlight the words or phrases that feel most like you. Perhaps give your report to one or two people who know you well. Ask them to do the highlighting activity; how do they see your strengths showing up? You may discover new information about yourself through your reflection and others' feedback on your strengths report.

There is no room for strengths envy

We are socially conditioned to focus on our own weaknesses, whilst admiring and sometimes feeling envious of the strengths of others. We may look at our colleagues, family and friends and think, 'I wish I had *that* as one of my strengths'.

There are two excellent reasons to ditch the envy. The first is that you can use your strengths to achieve the same strength as the one you envy. In coaching, people often ask, 'What can I do to improve what's at the bottom of my strengths list?'. I explain that for every strength in your bottom five, you have strengths in your top five that will do the same thing.

When I read my strengths profile for the first time, I was shocked (and indignant) to learn that empathy is not high on my list, even though I am an empathetic person. As mentioned earlier, I use a combination of other strengths to help me relate, care, and connect with others' experiences. I am genuinely curious about people, value deep connections, and want to learn.

The second reason to embrace your strengths is that every strength has a shadow side. For each strength you lack, you also avoid the challenges that go with it. Many empathic people find they take on other people's emotional load. They are highly sensitive to the mood or vibe of a group when they walk into a room.

As I don't have empathy as a dominant strength, I don't carry the baggage that goes with empathy and don't tend to take on other people's emotional stuff. Rather, I use my strengths to be curious, learn and build connections with people. These are all empathetic behaviours. I simply 'do' empathy differently without the shadow that can weigh down highly empathetic people.

How do your strengths make you *you*? How do they help you achieve your goals? How are they aligned with your values, and what is important to you? In what ways do your strengths energise and inspire you?

Remember that strengths are our lens for seeing the world. They are our filters for making sense of the information that comes our way. When we accept and embrace our strengths, we tell ourselves, 'I am enough, just as I am'. We do best when we focus our energy on Powering Up our strengths rather than fighting them and trying to change them.

'I always say that no single strength is better than another. No combination is better because all strengths are helpful in different situations. It's about getting people to broaden their thinking, rather than believing there is only one way to handle a situation.'

– Tanya Murray-Russell.

Recognising strengths in action

Once you have taken a strengths assessment, the next step is to reflect on how your strengths appear in your life. Tuning in to your strengths is a fabulous tool for firing up self-awareness. Just as you need to practice yoga regularly to get into a hot triangle or tree pose, you will need to put effort into getting to know your strengths. In my coaching work, I encourage clients to start this awareness building by focusing on their top five strengths for one week. Think of it as putting your strengths into the spotlight one at a time to see how they perform.

Notice how each strength shows up when it works for you and you get positive results. Also, note when it is working against you or stopping you from getting the best possible results. Here's an example to explain what I mean. I've included a template for this exercise at the back of the book.

It might be tempting to think of strengths as merely a useful tool, but that is not the full picture. Appreciate how each of your strengths can serve you and also get in your way. Understanding both sides of the story will offer deeper insights into how you show up in the world. It will help you understand how you behave under pressure or when you are fatigued. That is when we tend to use our strengths in the least disciplined way and are more likely to overuse or misuse them.

Overused strengths

Have you seen those lights that are adjustable with a dimmer dial? This is a great analogy for strengths. Turning the dimmer dial allows you to adjust the intensity of the light. Too low, and you can't see very far in front of you. Too bright, and you squint with discomfort. Either way, your vision is impaired.

Overused strengths are like the dimmer dial turned up too high. When we overuse a strength, it can seem overpowering. It takes up all the available space and crowds out our other strengths.

To the outside world, an overused strength can look like a weakness.

A fitting example of this is people who are naturally very adaptable. When this strength is adjusted to the right intensity, they can go with the flow and adapt to what is happening around them. When it is turned up too bright, they are so laid back that they are pretty much horizontal. They struggle to express a preference or viewpoint and can flip-flop when making decisions. They seem non-committal and unreliable.

Knowing when we overuse our strengths, what that looks like in action, and how it impacts our thinking and behaviour is incredibly useful. When we finally achieve self-mastery, we can objectively recognise and adjust these things in real-time and avoid the pitfalls of overuse.

Misused strengths

Used skilfully, strengths are like a tradesman's handy toolbox. Our dominant strengths are the tools we use most often and are most comfortable with. If you were a carpenter, your top strengths would be a hammer, saw, tape measure and chisel, and they would all be in tip-top shape, ready for use when needed.

When we misuse a strength, we grab the wrong tool for the job. We grab a chisel to bang in a nail. No matter how hard we hit that nail, the chisel is not the right tool. If you pick up the hammer and use it well, you will get the job done with minimum effort and maximum results.

> 'My strong positivity means that in almost every situation where there's a problem, I will be the guy trying to find a solution and drive it. When I misuse this strength, it shows up as naivety. Sometimes a thing is broken and no amount of positivity will fix it.'
>
> – Steve Klaassen.

Know your iceberg

Have you ever blurted something out in a conversation and thought, 'Where the heck did *that* come from?' Or you strongly reacted to something that came out of nowhere. Those blurts and reactions are not random. They are coming from your iceberg.

Edward T. Hall created the iceberg model to explain what happens in social groups – such as organisations.[2] The model can also be neatly applied at a personal level and helps us understand behaviour. Even better, you can take the insights and change your iceberg to get better results. Understanding how your strengths show up in your life will give you greater power over your iceberg.

We can deepen these insights by applying the iceberg model, which allows us to consider the thoughts, feelings and behaviours that show up when we use (and overuse) our top strengths. When we apply this model, we notice the hot buttons or trigger points that link our values, strengths, thoughts, feelings and behaviours. With practice, we can quickly change our outcomes by tweaking our strengths in action.

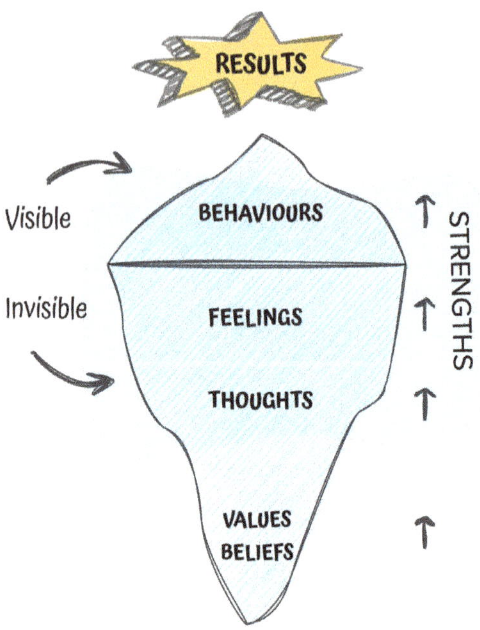

What does it all mean?

The results and outcomes we get rarely happen by accident. Think about a situation where you had some influence or control over events, whether it had a positive or unpleasant outcome. Your values and beliefs influence your thinking, emotions and behaviour and combine to create the outcome.

If you want different or better results, your iceberg is the place to start. When you add strengths into the mix, you can better understand how strengths influence perception and decision-making. You can use the iceberg tool in two quick ways: reflection on what has been and planning for what is ahead.

Look at your iceberg in the rear-vision mirror

Imagine you are driving away from a conversation. It might have gone exceptionally well, and you are feeling great. Alternatively, it might have gone badly, and you are sifting through the wreckage and wondering what derailed it. The iceberg gives you a framework to reflect more objectively on what happened and how your thoughts, feelings and behaviours contributed to the result. Adding a strengths lens enables you to name the strengths you called on in the situation. Whether the situation went well or pear-shaped, your strengths were in play. The important insight is how well they were used.

Look at your iceberg through your front windscreen

Now, imagine you are driving towards something you want to go well. It might be a difficult conversation or a challenging negotiation. Maybe it's a job interview or a performance review. Whatever it is, your iceberg can position you best for success.

Identify your goal: what is the best possible outcome you could achieve? What is the most useful mindset (thoughts) you could take into this situation, and how will that impact your feelings? How will that likely impact your behaviour and the results? Which of your strengths will help you achieve this mindset, emotional state and behaviour?

Up and down the iceberg

There are two ways to approach your iceberg – from the top down, starting with the results and your behaviour, or looking at values, beliefs and thoughts from the bottom up.

Starting with results gets you reflecting on or planning for behaviours and actions. The bottom-up approach offers a values-based perspective and considers how thinking has or can contribute to the eventual outcome of a situation. Each approach demonstrates how our strengths impact what is happening in our iceberg.

Return to the iceberg model as you work through this book and develop self-management and self-mastery. As you learn to use the right strength at the right time and with the right intensity, those iceberg insights will come more quickly and easily. Check with your iceberg in real time to supercharge interactions that are going well and get tricky situations back on track.

Understanding her strengths has helped Nicole Black manage her iceberg when setting expectations for herself and others.

> 'My future-focused strength allows me to have a clear vision and paint that picture for others to see. It's been a work in progress because it's so clear in my mind, and when I ask somebody to do something, I try to explain the result I want. When it comes back, sometimes it's not how I expected it to look. I've learned that if I am delegating a task, I need to be clear right from the start about what I want as an outcome.'
>
> **– Nicole Black.**

Nicole's example shows how her future-focused strength helps her see and share a goal. To get the best outcome, she knows her thoughts (I can delegate this task), feelings (optimistic for a good outcome) and behaviour (giving clear directions) need to align.

Hard conversations are a great example of putting the iceberg to work. I often work with teams that avoid talking about unmet expectations or misunderstandings. Such avoidance usually arises from the fear of conflict or confrontation. When these conversations do not happen, the result is often resentment, wasted energy and a loss of momentum. People spend too much time side-stepping issues or getting caught in a cycle of resentment and frustration.

You can avoid this if you are prepared to look at your iceberg. Reflect on what happened in the situation and what you could do differently next time by thoughtfully applying your strengths and intentionally tweaking your thoughts. Doing this will affect your feelings and behaviour and result in a different outcome. I have included the iceberg template at the back of the book for you to copy when you need it later.

Here's an example from a coaching client, Kasey. They were feeling increasingly frustrated and disengaged when it came to working on team projects. Their experience was that they were the only ones focused on getting project work done on time and in the most efficient way. When Kasey looked around the team, all they could see was others slacking off while Kasey was doing the hard work. When we first met, Kasey felt resentful, unmotivated and judgemental towards the rest of the team. It was reducing Kasey's productivity, and now their manager was asking some hard questions.

Kasey took a strengths assessment, and it was clear they had a strong sense of commitment and responsibility for getting things done. They also had some great relationship strengths, including empathy and kindness. Kasey could see that their resentment about shared work was getting in the way of good team relationships. We looked at the iceberg, and here is what Kasey wrote as a reflection (what happened this time) and to create a shift for the future (what I will try next time).

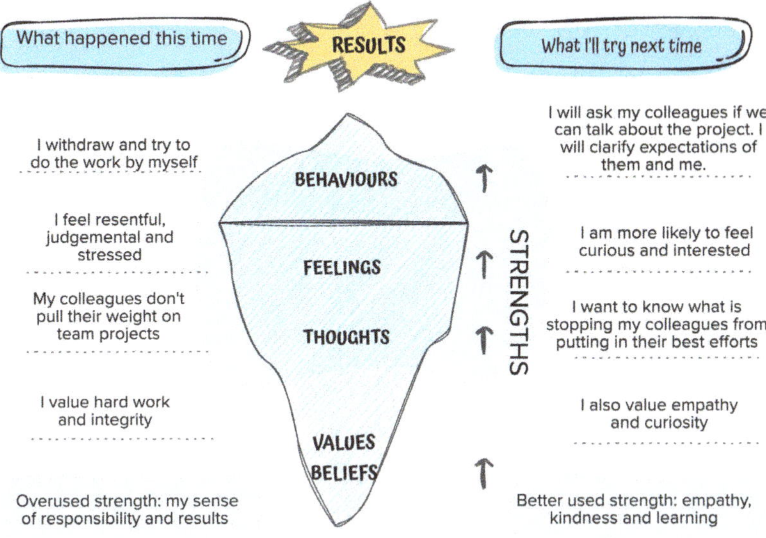

Using the iceberg as a reflective and planning tool, as Kasey did, is a brilliant way to increase your self-awareness. Over time, you will notice patterns in your thoughts, feelings and behaviours; we all have hot buttons or pressure points. When pushed, these set off the iceberg reaction. Learning to tune in when the button is pressed allows us to short-circuit the reaction. The more we practice applying strengths and interrupting that circuit, the better we will get at changing the outcome.

Next time you find yourself avoiding a conversation or frustrated that an interaction did not go to plan, be like a polar bear and check out your iceberg. Now that you are more familiar with your strengths and have developed strategies for noticing how they show up, it is time to build habits to put your strengths to work.

Letting your strengths glow

A campfire needs care so it does not burn out or get out of control. The best campfire for cooking anything, from dinner to marshmallows, has strong, glowing coals that give steady heat for a long time.

To let your strengths glow, you need to get into the habit of noticing and deliberately using them. I encourage my clients to create a simple strengths check-in for the days, weeks and months after discovering their strengths profile. Giving your strengths regular focus and attention will allow you to reach for them more naturally and easily. Here are my suggestions for creating a habit of noticing and using strengths.

BUILD A SUPERPOWERED HABIT

Write or print 3-4 copies of your strengths (business card size works well). Put these in plain sight on the fridge, bathroom mirror, computer & car dashboard.
Seeing your strengths will help you remember what they are, and tune your thinking into them.

Choose one of your strengths each week. Notice when you use that strength. Tune in to when it works for you (positive results) & against you (getting in the way of good results). Practise deliberately using each strength and notice the results.

Take half an hour to reflect on what went well in the past month. Think about how you used your strengths. Which were easier to use? Which took more effort? What results did you get?

Check in on your strengths.
How often have you used them? How has using your strengths impacted your energy and emotional state? Which do you use most often? Think of situations where you can use your strengths more deliberately.

If you want to make the most of your strengths, you cannot see them as set-and-forget. While it takes self-discipline and (at times uncomfortable) reflection, this habit becomes easier and more natural over time.

Start with a daily habit. Spend a week focusing on each of your top five strengths. Choose a different strength each week. That's five weeks of a daily habit of noticing how your strengths show up. Each week, notice how that strength shows up. What did that strength help you do? When did you overuse it?

Keep in mind that if you follow the process outlined in this book, you will be focusing on self-mastery by the time you get to the twice-yearly check-in. You will no longer be a strengths beginner. Instead, you will use your strengths deliberately and skilfully.

Talking up your strengths

Another great way to build a strengths habit is to share your strengths with others. Doing this forces you to put into words what your strengths look like in action. Talking about your strengths might be seen as bragging or talking yourself up. In Australia, it is common to downplay what we are good at and dismiss compliments when they come our way. We are much more likely to use humour to deflect praise and make light of our weaknesses.

Encourage others to give you feedback on times when you overuse or misuse your strengths. Inviting feedback is a terrific trust builder because it demonstrates vulnerability. Receiving feedback provides insights into how our strengths appear to others and opportunities to learn and grow. The information gained powers up self-awareness and self-management.

If talking about your strengths feels uncomfortable or even downright weird, here is some wording you could try.

'I've recently done a strengths assessment, and now I can put a name to my strengths and what they look like in action. If you see me doing X, it is just because of certain strengths. It is part of who I am and how I show up. I'm working on using my strengths more skilfully, so if you feel I am doing too much of that, let me know.'

Your Back Pocket Coach

Which of your strengths feels most like you? Which of your strengths puzzle you or make you curious?

Think of a situation where you are at your absolute best. Which strengths are you using well?

Describe what happens when you feel you are not at your best. Which strengths might you be overusing or misusing?

POWERING UP SELF-MANAGEMENT

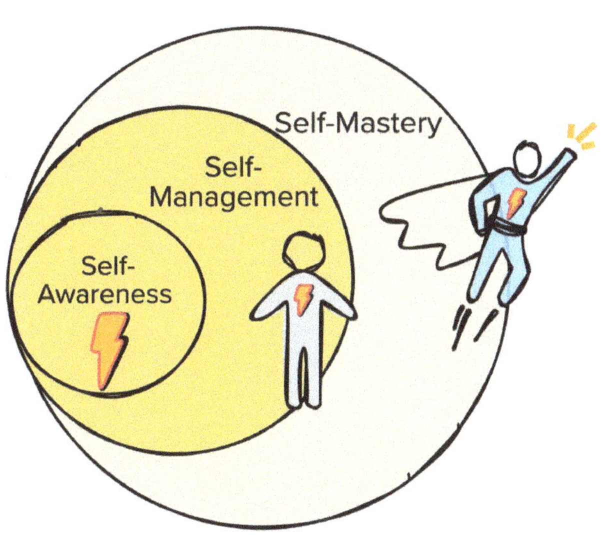

Manage thyself (before attempting to manage others)

What happens when The Hulk loses his cool? He turns bright green and his anger feeds his massive physical strength. He strikes fear into others, making them scream, run, stand and fight. He is a hero out of control.

In civilised life, we cannot afford to lose our cool. We must use our strengths to move from chaos to calm. And that takes practice. We might like to think we are thoughtful, rational creatures, but humans are emotional. We most often make quick decisions using the primitive part of our brain – the amygdala – the early warning system that lights up when we feel under threat.

Our brains were built to keep us alive by dodging predators and other physical threats well before we lived the life we experience today. The challenge is that human brains have not evolved to keep up, so we can experience social threats (such as not being accepted into a group) with the same intensity as facing a sabre-tooth tiger.

So far in this book, we have worked on self-awareness to better understand our hot buttons and what makes us behave as we do – especially under stress. Self-management allows us to take this knowledge and put it into practice. It allows us to self-regulate and respond, rather than react, to situations.

When we manage ourselves, we use strategies to pause and give ourselves time to work out our next steps. Without self-management we are like a pinball, rocketing from one situation to the next without control. Our emotions become the levers for our behaviour.

Applying self-management makes us more like the Marvel superhero Cyclops, who understands the value of a clear vision and focused attention to maximise his powers. Without his glasses, Cyclops' optic powers shoot everywhere. With his special visor, he can focus his beams of light and sight exactly where he needs them. Like any new skill, self-management takes focused attention and practice, making it easier and more natural over time.

Applying strengths skilfully

In the previous chapter, I discussed knowing your strengths and what they look like in action. I referred to strengths as the tools in your toolbox. When we apply strengths to self-management, we consider which strength will be most useful – which is the best tool for the job. Self-management allows us to notice when we are misusing or overusing a strength, adjust our use of it, or call on a different strength.

That may sound like a lot of effort, and yes, it initially takes practice. However, the habits of self-awareness and self-management mean that not only will it get easier over time, but you will also start to notice some amazing results.

For example, I have noticed that my brain loves to collect and share information. CliftonStrengths® calls this Input®. I explain it by saying my brain is like an old-fashioned filing cabinet. As I go about my life, random bits of information are gathered in the filing cabinet. People I have spoken to, books and news articles I have read, podcasts I have listened to, movies and shows I have watched. You get the idea. When conversing with someone, my brain is flicking through the filing cabinet, looking for anything useful that I might be able to share. It is something I do without thinking about it.

I love this strength; it helps me be a good coach and mentor. It is also helping me write this book! My Input® strength is totally fired up as I go through my mental files and share what I know.

Sometimes, though, this strength gets in the way of being a good listener, as my brain is busy in the filing cabinet. In a conversation, it can look like this:

> Me: How is that thing going with your new job? Is the team good to work with?
>
> Them: Yeah, it's going okay...everyone in the team seems tired and not working together. This remote work set-up is a real challenge. It'd be great to work out how to re-energise them and bring them together somehow.
>
> Me: (*Ding! I just heard a great podcast about this. There was an episode about this exact thing, so I should tell them about it.*) That does sound like a challenge. (*Is this the right time to mention the podcast? Hmm, I will wait and see.*) Are they aware of it and open to talking about it?
>
> Them: They're great people and seem to get along pretty well. A couple of them also seem nervous about sharing

their ideas. I wonder if they're worried about looking stupid. They're all smart people, so it'd be great to figure out what's happening. I want them to enjoy their work more.

Me: (*Ding! There is also an online article that could be useful. I must mention that, too.*) Hmmm.... Hey, there is a podcast and an article that could be useful for you to check out. I can send them to you if you would like?

That is me when I am not practising self-management, and my Input® strength is running wild. My brain lights up when it can find and share information that seems useful. The thing is, in that scenario, I missed the opportunity to really listen to the other person and acknowledge how they were feeling. They did not ask me to solve the problem. Chances are, they just wanted to be heard.

When our strengths are in overdrive, they can get in the way of building and strengthening relationships. We can also put our energy into something unnecessary. Rattling through the filing cabinet in my brain is fun, and it uses energy. If my suggestion or offer of information falls flat, I can feel disappointed, which takes more energy to process. I may leave that conversation feeling like I let the other person down by not being a better listener.

Self-management lets us notice when our strengths aren't being used well and adjust in real-time. This short-circuits that energy leak and the missteps we might make if we keep going down the same path. We can choose to use a strength more skilfully or a different strength better suited to the situation.

When I apply self-awareness, I hear *'Ding'* in my brain and notice that I am less present. At that point, I choose to put my Input® back in the toolbox and, instead, pick up my Learner® strength. I ask a curious question and listen to the answer. That helps me stay present and focus on the other person. They then experience me as someone who is genuinely interested and cares about what they have to say.

> 'It's powerful to turn particular strengths
> on in a context and flip between things
> you can use as the situation calls for it.
> You can switch strengths on and off.'
>
> – Kate Webber.

Self-management also allows us to notice and appreciate others' strengths. This happens because our reactions are often based on how we perceive them. When we find someone else irritating or perplexing, a great strategy is to put on our strengths goggles and see their behaviour through the lens of strengths.

> 'When particular strengths drive me up the wall, I
> know I have to make space for them and think, "This
> is just where their strength is different from mine".'
>
> – Tracy Duncan.

Managing your superpowers

In coaching sessions and workshops, I say, 'Remember, your strengths are your superpowers. You can use them for good and for evil.' (Wicked laughter added here for effect.) Self-management is about taking your strengths and using them in ways that work for you and help you achieve your goals. When strengths are our superpowers, we show up as the best version of ourselves.

One way to quickly get a sense of the shadow side of your strengths is to notice the results you are achieving. Are they what you are aiming for, or are you falling short?

> 'One of my superpowers is absorbing information and then putting it back into the world with my interpretation and value add. It's my Input®, working at its best. But when it gets out of control, I'm collecting shit for the sake of it. I'm just collecting gobs and gobs of articles, blogs and podcasts, and I'll lose track and create these avalanches of information for myself. Eventually, I have to tidy it up and sort it or ditch the stuff that isn't worth it.'
>
> – Christopher Miller.

Flexing our superpowers is not about changing who we are; it's about tweaking our behaviours to ensure our intentions and actions align. We want to leverage what we are naturally good at.

Tracy Duncan was a manager and mentor of mine. Her strengths show in her clarity of ideas and purpose. She has a talent for quickly seeing the big picture, identifying problems and forming solutions. She is an extremely quick thinker and moves rapidly from thought to action. People around her who enjoy problem-solving and getting stuff done, thrive. Tracy knows her strengths and welcomes feedback, even when it sounds like a backhanded compliment.

> 'My strengths mean that I am a confident communicator. I thought I was being nice all the time. I had no recollection or any clue that people would think any differently. Then someone pointed out that I was coming across in a way I wasn't aware of, and I'll always remember the feedback. Another manager told me, "You're not horrible at all." Why would they say that? When we talked it through, I realised that sometimes I was coming off as a know-it-all and bossy. I knew I had to deliver things a bit differently.'
>
> **– Tracy Duncan.**

Tracy is talking about her tendency for forthright communication. When she was aware of her impact, she adjusted her communication and managed her interactions for better results.

Managing the shadow side of strengths

Sandra Wood shared this great story with me about one of her coaching clients. Tom was a middle manager with a team of around 130 staff. After taking an online strengths assessment, he discovered that one of his strengths was fairness. Tom couldn't see how that could ever work against him, so he and Sandra looked at a recent project that hadn't gone to plan. Tom managed an office refurbishment, and the project went over time and over budget.

Sandra asked Tom how his strength of fairness might have contributed to the project issues. After some consideration, he had an Aha moment. He said, 'Well, I'm trying to interview everyone in the office and provide exactly what they need in their office refurb, so it's fair for everyone. I've spent so much time trying to give everyone what they need and want that the project has gone completely off track. I do that with other things at work, too, not just this. I tie myself up in knots, trying to please people and be fair so they get what they need.'

When Tom allowed his sense of fairness to run amok, it created chaos. The refurb project was a fitting example of the measurable and tangible impacts of overused strengths. Tom did not have enough budget for the promises he made, and his reputation took a real beating. He looked like an incompetent manager when all he was doing was trying to be fair to everyone. What I love most about Sandra's story is what happened next.

Tom learned to recognise the signs when his strength of fairness was switched on and starting to be overused. He learned how it felt in his body and to recognise the signals that he was tipping into dysfunction.He recognised an energy shift when he tried to accommodate everyone and knew when he needed to put better boundaries in place. That sense of being fair and using it as a strength made him feel solid and grounded. When it was overused, he was weak and wishy-washy. He became a people-pleaser.

When a strength is overused, there's almost an obsessiveness about it. Tom started to recognise that feeling and pull back.

Skilful use of our strengths means we can better manage our energy. Remember the WAVE model I introduced you to earlier? We get a surge of energy when we surf the strengths wave. Think of a time when you were doing something that came naturally to you and the next step seemed intuitive. Chances are you looked forward to doing that thing again, and it gave you deep satisfaction and energy. When we get energy from something, we use our strengths as superpowers.

When we overuse our strengths, we tend to create issues that need fixing. Tom spent so much time and energy consulting everyone, trying to be fair. What an enormous energy suck. He could feel the energy drain when he switched into overuse mode. It is likely that Tom also had to go back to people to explain that despite his best efforts, he could not meet everyone's requests, so he had to deal with unmet expectations.

Overusing strengths is a waste of energy. One of Sandra Wood's mantras is 'Value your energy like the precious resource that it is'.

Ultimately, would you rather your energy yield gold or a pile of dirt? Strengths will help you find the gold.

'I can become stressed and burnt out from
being an overachiever. My strengths also mean
I have to research until I have the full picture.'

– Donna Osmetti.

'Well, it's just burnout. Your expectations can
become too high; people can't live up to those
expectations. And part of the cycle is that I can't
expect them to do it, so I'll do it myself. I've learned
to delegate more and collaborate more with people.'

– Nicole Black.

Your Back Pocket Coach

For each of your strengths, take some time to reflect on the following:

What hot buttons or stress points are likely to trigger you to overuse specific strengths?

What are the consequences of overusing your strengths – for you and others?

POWERING UP SELF-MASTERY

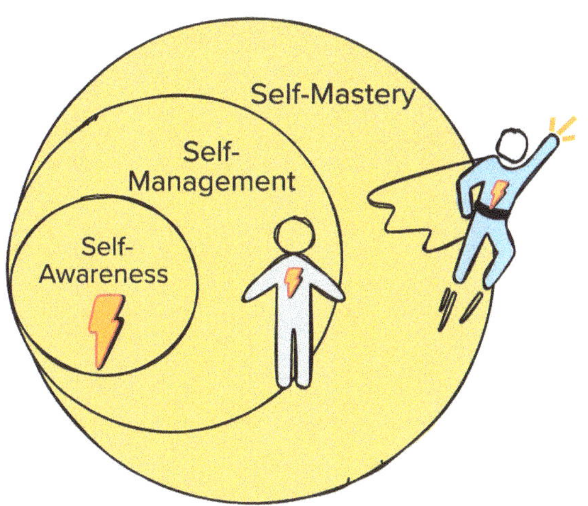

If you search for self-help and confidence boosters on social media, you will find endless inspirational quotes about being the best version of yourself every day. In my humble opinion, those words are pleasant but completely unrealistic. Some days we can be strong, confident and fire on all cylinders. We bring our

A-game to work, relationships and parenting. We go about life with seeming ease and grace.

On other days, we wilt and fold into ourselves. We sigh loudly, head down and shoulders drooping. Psychologically, we slump. We lash out, say the first thing that comes to mind, and bump up against others entirely wrongfully. Our emotions dictate our behaviour. These are not our best days and, honestly, they happen more often than we care to admit.

Self-mastery is like a fabulously smooth superhero onesie. It helps us suck in some of that emotional floppiness. It smooths out the lumps and bumps of our carelessly applied strengths. Self-mastery allows us to pull ourselves together and lean on our strengths, especially on the rougher days.

The ultimate power skill

Self-mastery is the ultimate upgrade when it comes to powering up strengths. It happens when we combine and build on that solid foundation of self-awareness and self-management. Self-mastery is evident when we deliberately and skilfully use the right strength, at the right time with the right intensity. When we are in self-mastery mode, we also appreciate and harness the strengths of others. In superhero terms, it is a Batman and Robin situation.

Strengths mastery is best summed up in this model.

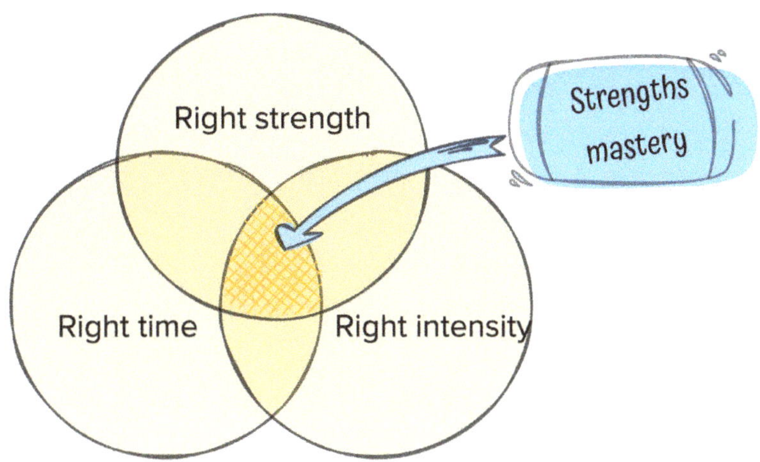

Right strength: You have a whole toolbox of strengths at your disposal. Not every strength suits every situation. Sometimes, using a particular strength can get in the way of success. Strengths mastery means shuffling through your strengths, working out which will best suit *this* situation, and choosing to use it rather than defaulting to whatever comes to hand. Remember, don't try to pound in a nail with a screwdriver.

Right time: Knowing when to use each of your strengths is critical. You might have to use a combination of strengths in any given situation. Some strengths are well-suited to opening a discussion or getting a task started. As the situation or task changes, you may need to use a different strength – one that is more suited to staying the distance or completing a task. You will want to use the right strength at the right time for the best result.

Right intensity: In the earlier section on overused strengths, I talked about dialling your strengths up or down, like a dimmer switch on a light. When you use a strength, you want to get that dial right. Sometimes, you might need to dial up the intensity – perhaps when presenting to your team or at a conference. You want to deliver a memorable, convincing argument that will have the crowd eating out of your hand. You are going to dial up those communication and relationship-building strengths. It might show in your animated face and big hand gestures. Your message will have high intensity and be attention-grabbing. Compare that to a quiet conversation with someone who wants to talk about their tough day at work or school. Chances are you will be sitting close to them, speaking quietly, and listening a lot. That's lower intensity.

Strengths mastery allows you to power up your strengths and help others do the same. When you combine these three elements, you are at your most aware, resourceful and skilled in harnessing the superpowers of strengths. Let's look further at self-mastery in action.

Powering up your strengths

It's entirely possible to deliberately choose the right strength at the right time. When coaching individuals and groups, I often share my favourite strategy for doing so. It sometimes involves recognising when another strength is getting in the way and must be swapped. I describe an action that involves mentally pushing down one strength and pulling up another. This is especially useful for visual thinkers.

When I spoke with Kate Webber about her experience attending one of my Starting with Strengths workshops, my push-pull example really stuck with her. I describe a situation where focusing on the future can drag you out of the present moment and how you might intentionally stay present by drawing on a different strength.

> 'You did a hand movement where you pushed down that future focus and pulled up your curiosity as another strength that can compensate when you find yourself in that zone. I've used that example in many other contexts because it's tangible and connected with me. I get very easily distracted by shiny new things, and it can manifest as me needing to be present for conversations. I catch myself by almost physically doing the action you demonstrated. I've got a name for this now, and I know what I need to be doing. When I use this strategy, I'm interested in what will come out of this person's mouth next.'
>
> – Kate Webber.

I love that Kate can now recognise, in real-time, when one of her strengths is getting in the way. She applies the push-pull strategy to power up self-mastery and shift the situation for a better result.

Helping others to power up

Self-mastery takes you beyond yourself. As the famous saying (almost) goes, 'No person is an island'. There is no denying that we get the best results when we use our strengths masterfully and help others recognise and use their strengths.

One of the best gifts you can give another person is to help them know and use their strengths. When you are powered up, I want you to go beyond your strengths and consider how to influence and partner with others. You have undoubtedly been riding that energetic lift that comes with harnessing your strengths. Imagine what you could achieve in your team, family or elsewhere if you could bring others along. Tandem strengths surfing anyone?

The first step in powering others up is to put your strengths goggles on. See if you can spot the other person's strengths. There will be clues in their behaviour and language. When you wear your strengths goggles, you interact with them more intentionally. You will be more curious and see them as having unique resources and talents. In short, they will be far more interesting than if you regard them through a deficit lens.

You can help others power up by asking them about their strengths. Be patient, as it might be the first time they have been asked. The WAVE model is a great way to explore strengths with someone. Ask what gives them energy and what they enjoy immersing themselves in. You will learn so much about them, and it is a great way to build relationships.

Lastly, explore where your strengths are similar and quite different. It is an excellent opportunity to explore how each of you sees the world, taking in and understanding information. These conversations allow you to construct a beautiful raft together, built on the mutual recognition of each other's uniqueness and tied together with the language of strengths to navigate the choppy waters that confront any relationship.

In the second half of the book, we will dive more deeply into helping others know and use their strengths. We will explore how you can share the secrets of powering up at work, in your relationships and helping others get through tough times.

Before we move on

I have created a handy checklist for you to assess your progress on the three elements of the Powered Up model. In each part of the model, we start with Warming Up and then, with practice, build to Powered Up. You might recognise other strategies and skills you have used more confidently. Make a note of these as well, as a way of reflecting and cementing your new Powered Up strengths habits.

	WARMING UP	POWERED UP
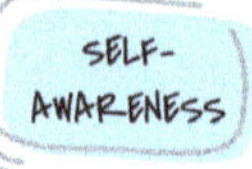 SELF-AWARENESS	Can name your strengths and how they show up in your decisions and actions. Deliberately practise the use of different strengths, much like flexing different muscles. Can recognise which of your strengths do the grunt work and are your go-to or most used strengths.	Notice, in real time, how you use specific strengths in different situations. You have developed strategies to tap into each of your strengths when needed. Know and can describe your impact when you skilfully use each of your strengths.
 SELF-MANAGEMENT	Identify hot button situations, such as when your strengths are switched on and overused or misused. Deliberately choose specific strengths in preparation for tackling certain tasks or interactions (playing to your strengths). Curious about other people's strengths.	Adjust the volume (intensity) of a strength in response to different situations. Shift gears in real time between different strengths relevant to the situation. Flip from judgement to curiosity (and empathy).
 SELF-MASTERY	Recognise and name others' strengths. Recognise the limitations of your strengths and see opportunities to partner with others. Identify and describe how each of your strengths can get in your way. Develop strategies to adjust how you apply them.	Give strengths-based feedback. Seek out strategic strengths-based partnerships. Make real-time adjustment for the right strength, right time and right intensity.

PART TWO

POWERED UP WORK

Bringing your strengths to work

How do you feel about your work right now? Do you bounce out of bed, excited for the day ahead and stride into work with a sense of enthusiasm? Or do you count the days (or even hours) until the weekend, plodding through your workdays with heavy shoes and a heavy heart?

It is unrealistic to believe we will always love all aspects of our jobs, but we can aim for a sense of purpose and value. Applying our strengths in targeted and skilled ways helps us do this. It can also shine a bright light on what we do best and be a source of confidence and an inner voice that says, 'You've got this!'.

Gallup® research shows that people who could name their strengths and use them at work were seven times more likely to feel engaged and satisfied by their work.[1] They were also three times more likely to perform 'very well' (according to their manager) and five times less likely to look for another job. To unpack that, people who know and use their strengths at work are happier, perform better, and more likely to hang around for longer.

In his book *Flourish,* Martin Seligman discusses the PERMA model for wellbeing, an acronym for the five measurable elements of Positive emotion, Engagement, Relationships, Meaning and Achievement.[2] As Seligman writes, 'You go into flow when your highest strengths are deployed to meet the highest challenges that come your way.' Flow is a state of complete engagement when we are fully immersed and preoccupied with a task. Seligman says that when we have all the elements of PERMA in our lives, we can flourish, and strengths are a critical ingredient.

> 'When someone uses their strengths to accomplish something, they are more energised and will get a better result. We describe strengths as being in the zone, where you can't help but do a particular thing, and the time goes fast. When people approach work from that place, there's a direct link to motivation, focus and quality of work.'
>
> – Sandra Wood.

You might choose to look elsewhere if you aren't flourishing in your current job or workplace. While flourishing doesn't need you to be in a job that is neatly aligned with your strengths, you also do not have to be in the perfect job to be happy at work. Wherever you are now in your work, there are many ways you can tap into strengths to boost your motivation, success and sense of satisfaction.

If you genuinely cannot see how your current job or workplace could allow you to flourish, a change might be needed. You can apply the following principles as you search for and settle into a new role.

The right tool for the job

Let's start with the big picture. While every job has its specialty area, my experience as a coach and manager suggests that four universal elements apply to any role. These are people, systems, organising and business skills. Understanding how we use our strengths in these areas provides shortcuts to apply them more deliberately. These are the tools of your trade.

Think about your strengths. How do you apply them for the best possible results? How could you use them more proactively or skilfully to improve your results? Make some notes about your observations. Be as specific as you can.

Bring your best self to work

Now that you recognise that strengths can be flexed to get results in particular work areas, how can you apply them to tasks or scenarios? For example, how do you bring your best self to a team?

I recommend a framework to create structure and discipline in sharing your strengths with others. This framework is great for explaining your strengths and is extra handy if you are applying for a job, asking for a pay rise, or describing how you contribute to a team. Don't hide your unique talents. Let them shine bright!

You're a superstar!

You may not realise this, but your superpower strengths make you a superstar! It is time to embrace your stardom; wear those strengths with pride and shout them out loud.

What do your strengths look like when used well? Translating strengths into practical examples makes it easier to talk about what you bring to the table at work, as the brain likes information that is easy to sort and classify. STARS creates a classification system to attach to your strengths.

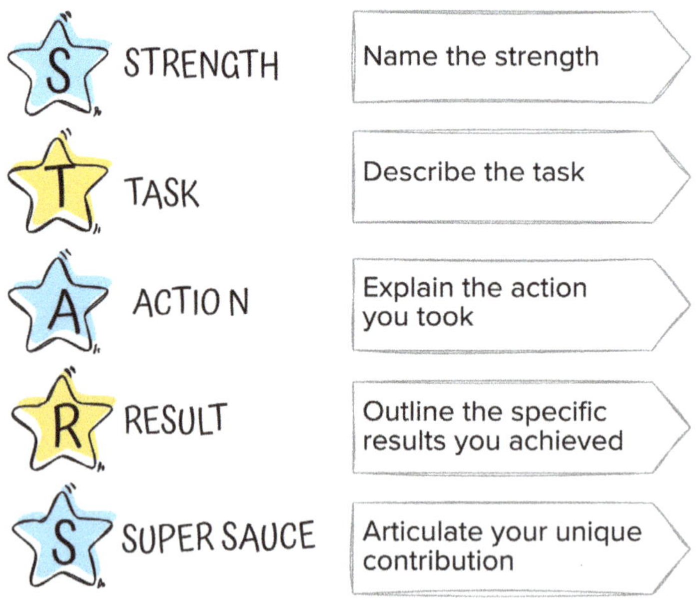

Let's apply the STARS framework.

Imagine you are preparing for a job interview. Think about what questions you might be asked and draw up STARS for each question. Now, you have prepared a logical answer and primed your brain, which will reduce any anxiety you might be feeling. Even without knowing the exact interview questions, you have done some groundwork and have useful information you can modify and adapt.

When you are in the interview, the people asking the questions will appreciate your thoughtful responses. Their brains will enjoy your logical, straightforward description of how you get exceptional results and make a positive impact.

Now, look at this in action. You have applied for a new job and been invited to an interview. Remember the four areas: people, systems, organising and business skills. Can you give a specific example of applying one of your strengths to one of these areas?

Here's an example of how someone might apply their relationship-building strengths in a people context.

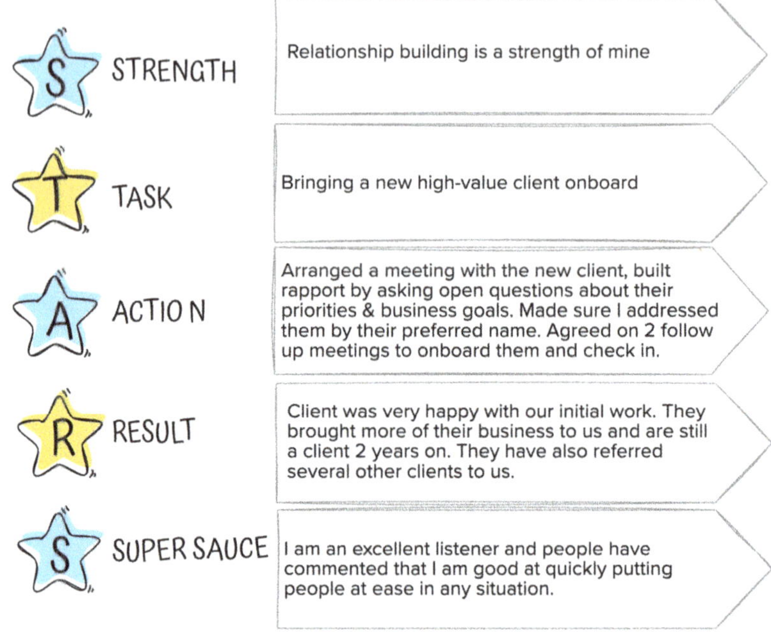

I've included a template of the STARS model at the back of the book. Copy it and note how you tackle the four core skill areas with one of your strengths. Try to use a different strength for each skill area. This will help you see how you use each of your strengths differently. It will also make you think about skilfully using each of your strengths to get different results.

Hot tip to power up self-mastery

Once a month, use the STARS template to reflect on the different strengths you have used. Keep notes so you have some solid examples to draw on when you are ready for that next career move.

'There's a significant alignment between my strengths and the things I enjoy that fill me up and give me energy. It has given me more confidence to own my strengths and talk about them in a way that helps me describe the value I could add to an organisation by using them.'

– Kate Webber.

'I have coached people over the years who are bored shitless in their job. They say things like, "I don't know how to (perform in an) interview", and have a lot of self-doubt. When they get their strengths report, and we work through it, I'm like, "There's your interview". You can put some facts to these strengths you have because this is where you do your best work. Now, they can find the language easily.'

– Mary Rezek.

Reconnecting to joy at work

You might be reading this and thinking that you don't feel you can use your strengths at work. That feeling of enthusiasm and connection might be missing or blunted by boredom, fatigue or even burnout. You might feel like one of those people Mary just described – a bit lost and plagued by self-doubt. The good news is that you can find or reconnect to joy anytime.

Start by looking for glimmers of STARS at work. You might not feel that your strengths burn bright at work, but there could be small, shiny spots here and there. Look closely at each of the four elements of work and identify any aspects that spark your interest. How could you do more to boost your satisfaction?

At the same time, consider which areas of your work you least enjoy and that seem to suck a lot of your energy. Clues to this include things you put off or procrastinate. How can you use your strengths in a targeted or different way to tackle those aspects of your work?

Another strategy is to think back to when you first started the job. What drew you to it? Was there something about it that felt exciting and challenging in a good way? Which of your strengths did this tap into? Is that still part of your job, or can you do something similar to reconnect with that feeling?

For example, I love learning; it's one of my strengths. When I start a new job or project, I get a real buzz out of the learning that comes with it. After being in a job for a long while, I can tap into my strengths to boost motivation by looking for new and different learning opportunities. These can be formal learning (enrolling in a workshop or training), researching and reading or talking to a colleague or expert who can teach me something new. Reaching for my love of learning gives me an energy hit and breaks up the monotony that can come with being in a job long term.

If you try these and still feel that you are not in the right job for your strengths (or other reasons), it's time for a new direction.

Rather than leaping into something different out of frustration or desperation, use STARS to help you prepare.

Now go back to the four core tasks activity. When and how do you use your strengths? What results do you get? What areas of work are you drawn to? Do you love facts and data, or are people and relationships more your thing? Consider the type of tasks and settings that you most enjoy working in. Look for roles that align with these qualities.

When our work is out of alignment with our strengths, it will likely take much more energy to feel engaged and satisfied. The ideal scenario is feeling energised, motivated and invested in what we do for most of our working hours. We care about the outcome and are willing to give our best efforts.

Applying our strengths to our work supercharges these efforts. Remember that misusing or overusing our strengths at work creates painful speedbumps on the way to excellent outcomes. By thoughtfully and deliberately using your strengths, you can transform a 'blah' working life into 'Brrrriiiiinnng it oooonnn!'

> 'Strengths help me create a brand for myself and sell that. A lot of us, particularly women, could be better at that. I'm an introvert and a nerd. I've had to learn to sell myself over the years.'
>
> – Tanya Murray-Russell.

Your Back Pocket Coach

Which of your strengths do you use at work most often?
How does it feel to use your strengths at work?

Which aspects of your work feel draining and less likely to engage your strengths? How could you intentionally apply your strengths to tackle these differently?

Strengths in teams

'After we learned about strengths as a team, people were kinder. They were more forgiving around the other staff members' needs and tried harder to communicate with them in particular ways. It was valuable work for us to do. Knowing our strengths helped to bring everybody onto the same page.'

– Kerry Grace.

That feeling of 'not being enough' or lacking confidence doesn't just affect individual performance; it hits teams hard, too. In an ideal world, we would all feel safe at work, admitting when we do not feel confident at the top of our game. Unfortunately, that is a somewhat rare scenario. When you gather a group of people at work, you also bring along a cartload of self-doubt and second-guessing.

Using our strengths skilfully as individuals allows us to get great results. Multiply this effect in a team and imagine what you could achieve. Can you recall a time when you worked in a team that lacked shared understanding about the task or goal? There was likely a lot of wasted time, and the air was thick with frustration. The amount of energy, effort and resources wasted in teams is astounding. Yet, teams are too close to the action to see what is happening. The feelings are real, but the insight is lacking.

Strengths can help a team decode challenges and opportunities. Think of it like an escape room. Each person brings their style of problem-solving and clue-breaking. Some people are logical thinkers; others are more creative and interpretive. You need all the different styles to solve the various puzzles and make your way out of the room. Ideally, you will leave as friends with a sense of achievement and pride.

What is your goal for the people in your team? Do you want them to feel excited and energised by their work and able to contribute what they do best? It doesn't take an expert to know you will get far more from people when they feel this way.

My colleague Mary and I recently worked together to deliver an online workshop to a group of fellow consultants. I was excited to work with Mary because she is a highly experienced coach and consultant. Mary specialises in working with big teams in government and private enterprises, and her energy and passion for her work beam through our Zoom calls. We have different strengths and I was curious to understand how she experienced our joint project. I love Mary's direct, no-bull communication style. Here's what she said when I asked about our work together.

> 'One of the things that I appreciate about you, Nicole, is that you get shit done. My being "now" and in the moment is different from yours. Your now is, "Okay, this is what I need to do. I have all these things in motion, I have to get this done, and I'm going to do it really well". And BAM, it's off your desk! Whereas I'm like, "Oh, okay, so I need to noodle around. I need to take my time to edit it". When I need to go into action, my "now" is the physical action. Structure sets me free, and you provide structures to play with. Give me a blank piece of paper and I'm going to stare at it. When you initiated and put a start together, I could co-create.'

Mary's snapshot describes two people coming together and using their strengths. We were both able to work in ways that suited each of us, and we got the job done. Her telling of the story might sound like Mary is less organised than me, but that is not true. We simply have a different sense of what is immediate. Mary loves to work 'in the moment'.

> 'I don't have goals. Even within my business, every time that I've tried to set a plan or a goal, everything blows up. I can't see my way out of a paper sack for two weeks. But I can plan for my future by knowing I need to care for myself when I'm 85, so I'm building a house. How I get there is quite organic.'

I am a natural planner, so I find Mary's lack of need to have the future all worked out puzzling, but I can respect it. Understanding this about her helped me tailor my approach to our shared project. I understood that my brain could relax if I did what came naturally to me and put together an overall workshop plan well in advance. I knew Mary would get involved and excited closer to the workshop delivery date. In those last few weeks, her excitement kicked in. She asked insightful questions, made suggestions and had valuable ideas from her experience. I learned so much from her, and the workshop went without a hitch.

When you think about the most successful team you know, what do you imagine people are doing? Does each team member slouch in and bring a half-hearted effort? Are they bored and distracted? Obviously not. High-performing teams bring out the best in people. They bring energy, motivation, and a sense that 'we can tackle anything'. It is a no-brainer that when people bring their best to a team, they use their strengths. The recipe for a successful team is more than just the individual contributions of each team member. It is about the culture created by knowing and using their strengths.

I asked coach and consultant Christopher Miller what he has noticed when working with teams. He said:

> *'Strengths create a level of mutual respect. Suppose you can identify a complementary partnership or a trio of people who work well together. In that case, you can say, "We work so well because one of us has the ideas, someone else is a born implementer, and the other person is the relationship builder.*

We know what role we play. We can all play each other's role when needed, but we play best when we stick to our own roles.'"

When teams recognise each others' strengths, they focus on the unique value each person brings. They also appreciate that team success relies on everyone, not just one or two people.

Christopher explained that when we know ourselves well, we can show respect to our team members by using our strengths skilfully.

'As an ideas person, I pick my best three ideas and present those weekly. No more than that because if I don't discipline myself with generating and sharing ideas, I'm just going to flip out the implementer in the team.'

In this team, the members are not merely bringing a strength to the table; they are choosing to use the right strength at the right time, with the right intensity. Thank you for a beautiful example of self-mastery in action, Christopher!

Curious teams

Personally, I would choose a curious, open team over a highly skilled but closed-down team any day of the week. Powering up strengths in teams starts with discovery and sharing. Each team member completes a strengths assessment and considers the results. Everyone needs to tap into their superpowers.

When it comes to sharing, a great approach is for each person to read their strengths report and highlight the words or phrases that seem most like them. They also give their report to one or two other team members and ask for feedback. Which words or phrases do they think best describe the person? How do team members see each other's strengths showing up?

When I coach teams, I create a strengths grid, which maps out the strengths of all team members in a matrix. The grid is a terrific visual tool for helping teams appreciate shared and different strengths.

An important activity in sharing strengths is hearing each person's unique experience. While people might share a particular strength, how this shows up in their work can be quite different. Our strengths work together as a collective toolkit to shape how we show up and thrive. By asking people about their unique strengths, we're saying, 'I'm interested in knowing the real you'. What a powerful relationship builder!

To avoid labelling people according to their strengths, I encourage teams to ask curious questions to learn more about one another rather than making assumptions. For example, instead of saying, 'Oh, I can really see your empathy in this situation', a better approach is asking, 'Which strength do you think is kicking in for you in this situation?'.

This question is especially helpful for people with similar strengths. It can be easy to assume that others experience a strength as we do. For example, one of my strengths is that I love to network and connect with others. Doing this gives me a real fizz of energy. In CliftonStrengths®, this is called WOO® or Winning Others Over. I especially love this strength because it allows me to enjoy meeting new people, building my network and connecting like-minded people.

I have met others who share this strength. For some, my energy and network-building skills for connection are bang on. For others, it feeds into their abilities as salespersons, a role I happily run a mile from. The lesson from this is that to truly appreciate one another, we need to be open and curious.

Asking curious questions means regularly providing opportunities to think and discuss our strengths. It helps us build and nurture a strengths-based culture in the team and prevents us from falling into bias or assumption traps, where we interpret others' behaviour through our own lens.

> 'When you map the team's strengths, you're suddenly looking at each person around the table as somebody who can complement what you bring. Doing that mapping also allowed us to connect, bring people together, and foster a collaborative culture.'
>
> – Kate Webber.

Trusting teams

Trust builds and sustains relationships of all kinds, while the lack of trust can damage and even destroy them. When trust is low, we spend a lot of time and effort protecting ourselves from each other, which slows down the team and hinders success.

People will still understand your meaning and intention if you say the wrong thing in a high-trust relationship. In a low-trust relationship, you can put a lot of thought and effort into your communication and still be misinterpreted or misunderstood. Stephen R. Covey likens trust to an emotional savings account.[3] If you have built up a healthy balance of trust over time, you can make some withdrawals (missteps) along the way. If there is nothing in the savings account, there is nothing to draw on.

Trust crushers

Like taking a hammer to a window, some behaviours are a surefire way to inflict damage to a relationship. When trust is damaged or broken, it can be difficult, if not impossible, to recover. When I work with teams, I often use the phrase, 'What you ignore, you accept'. I've paraphrased Lieutenant-General David Morrison AO, who said, 'The standard you walk past is the standard you accept'.[4] Accepted behaviour defines your team culture. If trust crushers are ignored, your team says, 'It's okay to behave that way around here'. Every team member is responsible for acting with care and calling out poor behaviour. Trust builders help create an environment where it is safe to call out poor behaviour and resolve the underlying reasons.

Trust builders

Every relationship and interaction with a person, company, product or service is based on three elements: expectations, needs and promises. One way to think about trust is to imagine a wall. Vanessa Hall has a handy trust model that uses this analogy.[5] She says trust relies on our belief that our expectations will be met or managed, our needs will be met and promises made to us will be kept.

Imagine that our expectations and needs, and the promises others make are all bricks in this wall. Some bricks will be more important than others. For example, our expectations include being paid on time and having regular meetings with our manager. We also expect reasonable people to work with and positive work relationships. Here are some other bricks in the wall of trust.

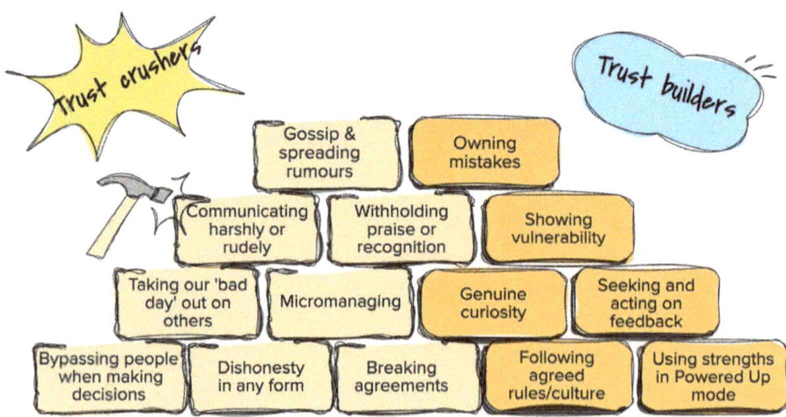

You can see that one of the foundation bricks uses strengths in Powered Up mode. Working skilfully with strengths means we are more in tune with ourselves and others. These are big trust builders. When we see people's strengths and invite them to work in their most natural ways, we embrace diversity. We step away from the idea that there are right and wrong ways to do things. Instead, we explore how each team member can get the job done in a way that aligns with their strengths.

Productive teams (AKA teams that get sh*t done)

The beauty of strengths is that we all bring something different to the table. When we use our strengths, we are at our most productive. A talented team knows how to harness the best of each person to create a powerful combination of skills, passion and energy. Think of the action/adventure movies *The Avengers* and *Justice League*. These crews of superheroes knew that to disarm a common threat, they needed to combine forces, with each bringing their unique superpowers. Your team goals do not have to involve saving humanity from an evil power or incoming asteroid.

We waste too much energy trying to do things that are not in our wheelhouse. For example, I don't love data. There is minimal cross-over in a Venn diagram between what data analysts do and what I do. My motivation and energy take a nose-dive if I am faced with a spreadsheet full of numbers. I have to work super hard to stay engaged and achieve anything. If someone was to pay me to do that, they would be wasting their money. Yet there are many people (I know some of them!) who love nothing better than to make sense of numbers.

Now, amplify this to team level. How many people are doing tasks they are unsuited to? How is that impacting productivity? Your team strengths grid and robust conversations will help you determine how to assign work for the greatest benefit to all.

Does that mean the team will be 100% productive? No, that is unrealistic. Does it mean team members only do work aligned with their strengths? No, that's also unrealistic. We want to create the best possible alignment of tasks to the strengths available in the team. We then assign the other work according to logical workflow, experience and skills. If there is truly no one in the team to assign that task, it is time to look at contracting out.

> 'As a leader, I look at each person's strengths
> and use them to motivate them and help
> them achieve their best. My colleagues have
> strengths that are different from mine, and
> holistically, we all come together as a team in
> a way that benefits everyone we work with.'
>
> – Donna Osmetti.

'There's limited value in investing in areas that
I'm never going to be amazing at when I could
look to the person beside me who brings that
to the table and really focus on what I can do.
Recognise that if you are particularly amazing
at something, there's incredible value in
specialising and being known for that skill.'

– Kate Webber.

'Because I knew my strengths, I could better see
others' strengths, allowing me to match the best
people to projects we needed to get done.'

– Peggy Webb.

When you know your team members' strengths, you can apply them more deliberately and decisively to a task. That is where Strengths Mastery is valuable at a team level. Remember, it's about using the right strength, at the right time, with the right intensity.

Think about a team project you are working on. It might be business as usual or a one-off piece of shared work.

The *right strength* is all about which team members are needed. Different strengths, and therefore different people, are needed.

The *right time* relates to when different project stages need particular strengths. For example, at the start of the project, you may need people who are great instigators, designers, planners and strategic thinkers. Later in the project, you will want people whose strengths relate to finishing things and checking the details.

The *right intensity* is all about the volume you need from the strengths. Say you have many stakeholders to keep informed through meetings, emails, newsletters and social media updates. This is a job for someone with communication strengths who will happily pump out those messages.

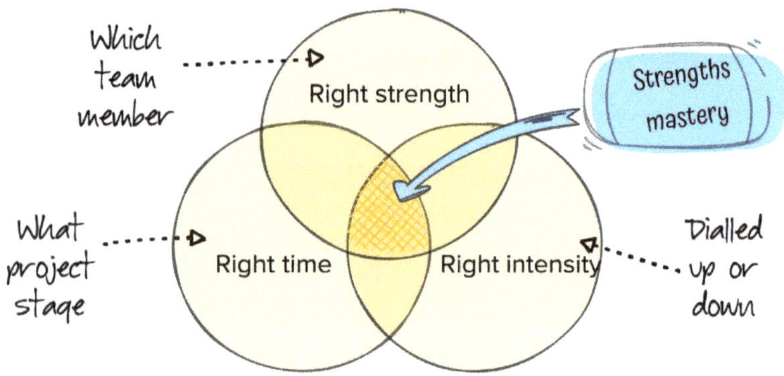

A team can set itself up for success by creating a clear picture of their vision, purpose and shared goals. This is only part of the story. When you introduce strengths into the mix, you are supercharging the opportunity for success. The best news is that people feel valued for their unique brand of productivity. Instead of feeling worn out by work, they are energised and invested in the results.

'When you bring people with different strengths to the table, you get a much better product, outcome or output. It's about genuinely appreciating and valuing the strengths of others and inviting them to the table in a very specific way. It's not just about saying, "We should collaborate on this", but rather, "Hey, we need you because of your strengths".'

– Tanya Murray-Russell.

'I get energised by working with people, motivating people and mentoring people. I'm good at laying down the vision and how we will get there. I focused on building my business administration skills, which I'm not good at. I don't enjoy it, but I need to have that to be able to achieve what I want. But I've got many other great people around me with those skills. It's liberating that I don't need to do it all.'

– Nicole Black.

If you did not have to earn an income, how would you want to contribute to your community?

What is the special sauce or unique value you bring to a team because of your strengths?

When are you at your best at work? What tasks are you happiest doing?

What do you wish your work colleagues knew about your strengths?
What does your supervisor or manager need to know about you to get the best from you?

Leading and influencing with strengths

How do you show up as a leader? More to the point, how do your *strengths* show up in how you lead? Many people I coach come to me confused and frustrated because, despite their best intentions, their efforts as leaders are not getting the results they need. In almost every case, the problem is not a lack of skill; most often, it's overused strengths creating speedbumps and barriers. These leaders are getting in their own way.

'I want to have people with all the different skill
sets that can complete the puzzle. And we deliver.
I play to all my teams' strengths and assign them
work that meets that – because it's in their interest
and mine. When we can't do that, we have to work
together and share those bits so we can deliver.'

– Tracy Duncan.

How often do you say to yourself, 'I should be more of this or more of that'? Our inner voice is often full of judgement. That voice can be a real energy suck. It also induces a lot of second-guessing, leading to indecision and low confidence. But what if that voice was informed by what you are good at and encouraged you to enjoy more of that?

'I struggle to get out of the trenches as I like
managing projects, not people. Knowing
that about myself through my strengths
helped me to forgive myself a little bit.'

– Kerry Grace.

Within your strengths profile, you have the keys to unlock your toolbox of leadership superpowers. Leadership does not have to be loud and brash. It can be quiet and unassuming. There is no ideal strengths profile for every leader. You can turn your superpowers towards whatever task you are passionate about, including setting a vision and inspiring others to go with you. I believe you will be a far more successful leader by being authentic and leaning on your strengths, than pretending to be someone you are not.

The idea machine

One CEO I worked with was keen to know how she could move from being operational to a more strategic leader. She was keen to delegate more and encourage her middle managers to step up and take on stronger leadership roles. We met as a group to discuss what needed to happen to achieve this change.

As is often the case, the middle managers talked about having a heavy workload and needing more clarity on the priority of tasks delegated to them by the CEO. One of the CEO's strengths (and passions) was creating new ideas and opportunities for the organisation. She often shared those ideas and opportunities in meetings and emails.

The middle managers talked about being flooded with emails about a particular topic, wondering which direction they should be heading and then realising the CEO was on a brainstorming jag. There needed to be a system for assessing priorities or what they should do with the information.

As I worked with the team, it was clear that they needed a process to allow the CEO to share her ideas without overwhelming or side-tracking the team from their core work. We created an online parking space for the CEO to store and categorise the information.

The team could then visit the parking space when it was relevant, such as before a meeting when a particular idea or opportunity was on the agenda. This system provided clarity for the team. It also meant they could see what might be coming down the pipeline of work projects and align their efforts with that.

One of the middle managers told me that seeing what was in the parking space meant he did not take on the mental load of juggling a lengthy list of half-baked ideas. It also meant he could focus on ensuring they had systems and processes supporting emerging ideas, moving the team from a reactive approach to a much more proactive one. Clarity, structure, communication.

Giving feedback

> 'Using the language of strengths takes the heat
> out of a difficult conversation. It's a remarkable
> tool to be able to say to somebody, "I feel like
> you're over-utilising a strength". It's a much
> more empathetic way of delivering feedback,
> giving insight to people and coaching them.
> And people respond really well to it.'
>
> – Kate Webber.

For the love of all that is good, never, *ever* use the feedback sandwich. You'll recognise it as a management technique from the 1980s. It is unclear who created this approach, but it is now widely considered a confusing and unhelpful way to give feedback.

The feedback sandwich involved saying something complimentary, giving critical or negative feedback, and finishing with something complimentary. Here is what it looked like in action: 'Hey, Frankie, thanks for getting that report to me so quickly. It was some of your best work. I noticed you came in late this morning, though. Don't let it happen again. We always appreciate your efforts in the team, so keep that up.'

Frankie would have two possible responses. Either they heard all the good stuff and the issue about being late to work was lost, or they were completely confused about the conversation and walked away none the wiser. In the worst-case scenario, Frankie only heard the comment about being late to work. There was no opportunity to clarify why they were late, and now they are wary of any conversation with their boss.

At its heart, the feedback sandwich is an excuse for managers to avoid discomfort. While they tell themselves they are softening the blow of a hard conversation, it is more about their awkwardness or lack of confidence in dealing with a difficult topic.

Ditch the feedback sandwich and replace it with feedback SUITS. Here's how to do it.

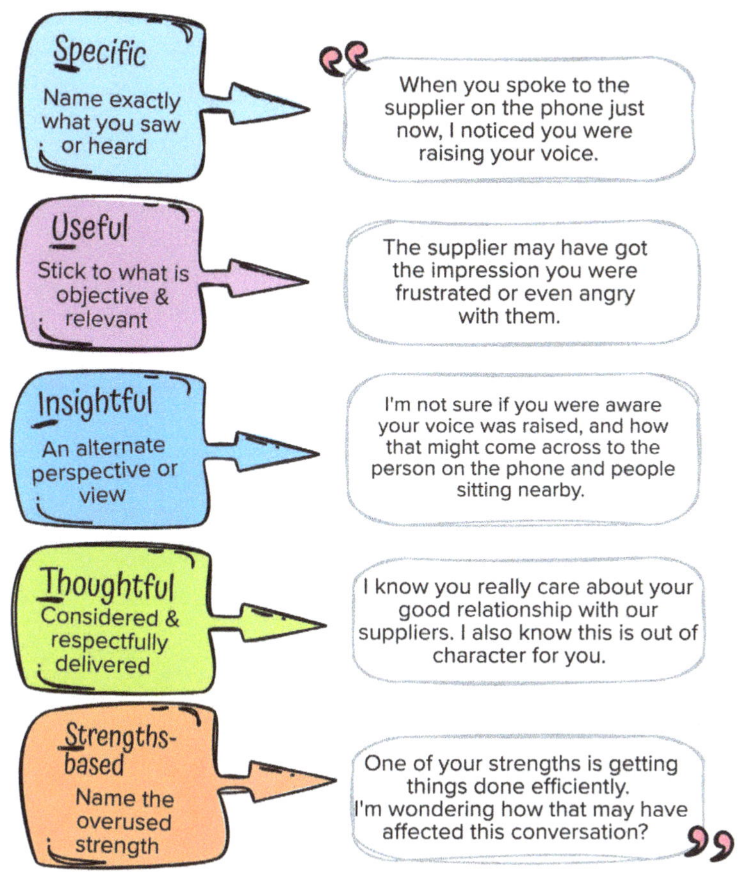

Name the strength the person is misusing or overusing and ask which strength might be more helpful. Encourage them to identify their own strengths. If they struggle with this, pinpoint one of their strengths to get them started.

'When you start a (critical) feedback conversation with strengths, it's like switching on the hazard lights on your car. You can stop and park where you need to, to give people feedback. Strengths allow you to do that in a non-threatening way so people don't instantly feel defensive.'

– Steve Klaassen.

I worked with a leader who came to me about Carlo, an underperforming member of their team. The entire leadership team in this company was committed to helping Carlo lift his game. They could see he had excellent skills and values aligned with the company's purpose. The challenge was how to get a significant boost in his performance within a short space of time. They wanted to have a 'tough but transformative' conversation with him to turn things around.

Around the same time, the entire leadership team had done a strengths workshop with me. They arranged for Carlo to do the CliftonStrengths® assessment as well. They believed that strengths could play a big part in resolving this challenge.

Carlo's manager came to me a short time later and told me that it was clear that Carlo was simply in the wrong role; his strengths were much better suited to different work. He ran on a mouse wheel of poor performance and demotivation, each feeding the other. This decimated both his confidence and the belief others had in him.

The manager found an operational gap in the organisation, designing and delivering consistent, high-quality staff training. This work played to Carlo's strengths. He had deep knowledge of the company and the processes staff needed to follow. He was passionate about helping others develop their skills. The kicker was that the manager avoided this work because it did not fit her strengths.

This story is an excellent example of a company recognising that each person has valuable strengths. Poor performance needs addressing, and an important first step is to determine whether the person is overusing or misusing strengths. It is also important to consider whether a team member's role utilises their strengths and engages their interest. People rarely go to work thinking of ways they can perform poorly. Adopting a strengths lens shifts our thinking from the blame game to the A-game. It allows us to ask what this person does well and how to align that with the work.

Turning teams around (so they can get great sh*t done)

In my experience as a coach, turning performance around is the number one challenge for most people leaders. Whether it is a single player on the team not pulling their weight or a culture of poor performance, that stuff needs to be tackled. Having tough (or courageous) conversations to challenge poor performance can feel tricky.

A strengths culture creates the space to shift discussions about poor performance away from a deficit or blame approach. It is far more productive to talk about how a strength has been overused or misused, which deepens insight into behaviour. The conversation can then focus on applying strengths to get better results in the future.

This approach works with individuals and groups. Anyone can use these principles in a one-to-one discussion or a group meeting about improving performance.

One of the most satisfying coaching discussions I've had was with a senior teacher. Jamie (not her real name) had recently been promoted and had gone from being one of the team to the leader of the team, which created a few challenges. One of Jamie's key frustrations was the general culture of complacency when it came to submitting student reports. Twice a year, in June and November, each teacher had to submit completed academic reports for all their students.

Jamie's bugbear was that the teachers in her team submitted reports late – despite repeated reminders and requests about the deadline. The reports were also of poor quality. Jamie's response varied from cajoling (verging on begging) to spending nights and weekends correcting the reports herself.

My question for Jamie was: Which of your strengths are getting in the way of you holding these people accountable? You have set clear deadlines and expectations. They are adults. What do you think is going on?

After a thoughtful discussion about her strengths in action, Jamie identified two overused strengths. Empathy® and Harmony® (the peacekeeper) meant Jamie only saw the situation from her colleagues' point of view. She could empathise with their stress at report time. As a natural peacekeeper, Jamie's view was that accountability equalled conflict. She perpetuated the problem by correcting the reports herself.

To turn things around, Jamie needed to have honest discussions with the team's poor performers. So, we talked through which of Jamie's strengths could be most useful in tackling these conversations. Jamie decided she could use Developer®, a strength that recognises and nurtures the potential in others. By adopting that lens, Jamie could see the people on her team as learners and accountable adults.

Jamie's story could apply to any leader. Holding people accountable and having critical conversations can be daunting. A great starting point is to consider which strengths could get in the way of having the conversation. Next, consider which of your strengths might help you gain a different perspective on the performance issue, the person, or both.

When we shift to a strengths lens (I call it putting on your strengths goggles), we change how we start the conversation, how we connect with the other person and the results we get. You will feel less combative and stressed, and the other person will have a much more positive experience of discussion than they otherwise might have. Your mantra? Go from *stressed* to *strengths*.

> 'When we take a strengths approach, we can talk about (performance issues) more in the third person, allowing for a broader discussion. It feels less like a personal attack. You start by acknowledging their strengths and talking about the strengths in action. Then, you ask them to self-assess where they did or didn't apply the strength. It's the opposite of "You stuffed up", which must mean you are a stuff up.'
>
> – Steve Klaassen.

> 'If you can address an issue or behavioural issue from a strengths base, they're much more likely to be open to the feedback and then much more likely to change their behaviour. In a way, it's affirming them and then requesting an adjustment of strength rather than saying, "There's something wrong with you".'
>
> – Sandra Wood.

Flipping the narrative on poor performance

I want to finish this chapter with a simple strengths hack that will give you a new perspective on poor performance. I'm talking about low-level concerns like time wasters who draw colleagues into lengthy conversations or team members who dither around with a project rather than finishing it and moving on. These issues can be considered poor performance or misunderstood strengths.

When we view behaviour through a strengths lens, we can flip the narrative and look for the strength at play. I have listed some common traits that are sometimes perceived as weaknesses and their corresponding hidden strengths. These are examples only, and when faced with challenging behaviour, I encourage you to ask curious questions to explore the strength behind the behaviour.

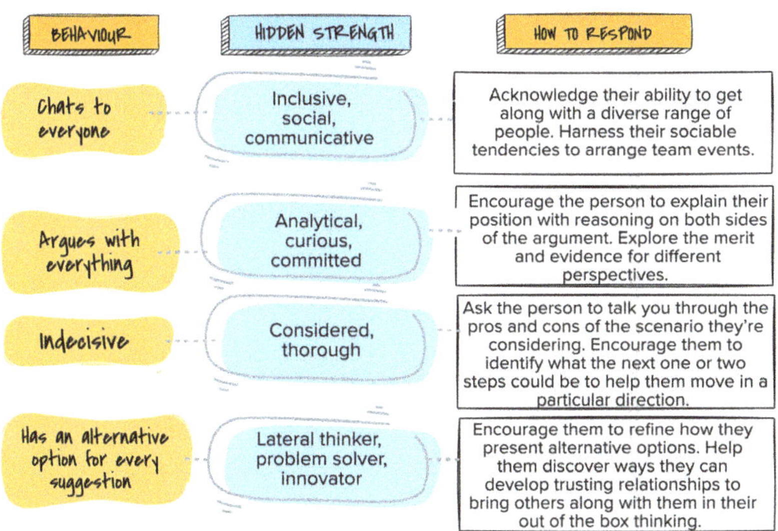

Your Back Pocket Coach

How would you describe your leadership style? How do your top five strengths show up when you influence and lead others?

Which of your strengths do you lean on most as a leader?
Which of your strengths are most challenging to use as a leader?

If you had to talk to someone about poor performance at work, which of your strengths would be beneficial in that conversation? Would any of your strengths be a challenge?

POWERED UP CONNECTION

Relating with strengths

For the past 85 years, Harvard researchers have followed a group of 2000 people in a lifelong study into happiness.[1] The researchers want to know what makes a good life. It turns out the answer is not money or career success. Close relationships and social connections are crucial for our wellbeing. Having supportive and nurturing relationships buffers against life's stresses and protects overall health.

What can we learn from this study? The researchers suggest that we boost our wellbeing through relationships right now. You can start with a stocktake and ask yourself, 'Who do I have a relationship with right now? What am I getting from the different relationships in my life?'

We get different things from different relationships. Some relationships give us fun. Some relationships include confidants.

Some relationships include my neighbour, who loans me their lawnmower when I need one.

So, the first thing is to consider your relationship world and ask, 'What am I getting right now? What do I have enough of? What would I like more of? Is there a way to strengthen some relationships I already have, or is there a way to make some new connections?'

Where do strengths fit in?

Steve is an industrial relations specialist who has made a career out of finding ways to get the best from people. He has attended a lot of professional development and never expected to find something at work that would be just as helpful at home.

'Learning about my strengths is the only session
I've been in where I can take that away and
apply it to the most essential parts of my life –
relationships, family, friends and understanding
my decisions in my personal life. The fact that
I can put it into practice across all the parts of
my life is a big part of what I like about it.'

– Steve Klaassen.

Whether you're in a brand-new relationship or something that has been steady for a long time, bringing strengths to the table can transform a connection from flatlining to heart-pounding. I realise that is a big call, but here's the thing: strengths will give you insights into your connections in ways you have not imagined.

Something that thrills me and surprises many of my workshop participants is the universal benefits of strengths. That is my fancy way of saying, 'Use your strengths everywhere in your life!' The more you practice them, the better results you will get. Use them at home or with the sporting team you are part of or the craft group. Practice strengths spotting with your family and friends. Keep building those strengths muscles!

Who we connect with

There are relationships in our lives that we choose and those we find through birth, work, school, or other associations. These relationships can be a source of nurturing or frustration – sometimes both at once. You might not be able to choose your family, but you can choose how any relationship affects you.

We play different roles depending on our relationship with different people. I have watched people I thought I knew well shift and change like a proud chameleon. They adapted to their various roles depending on who they were with.

The roles we play include:

- family (child, sibling, etc)
- romantic partner
- parent

- friend
- associate by proximity (neighbours, etc)
- professional associate.

Regardless of *who* we connect with, our strengths influence *how* we connect with them. Think about how your strengths show up in your relationships. What matters most to you when it comes to relationships? Is it having a wide circle of friends, deep connections with a small group of people, or perhaps both? Consider how your relationships allow you to use particular strengths. Are there relationships where using your strengths is more challenging?

How we connect

Are your relationships on autopilot?

Think about the positive life-changing or life-shaping events in your life. These are the experiences that have stuck with you. Chances are, in those situations, you were not alone. Other people were there with you. Setting our relationships up for success means taking positive steps to connect and care for ourselves and others, and we cannot do this on autopilot.

In his book *Thinking Fast and Slow*, David Kahneman encourages us to think about our brains as having two different thinking systems.[2] The first is fast and intuitive. The second is slow and analytical. We make thousands of judgements every day as we take in the world around us and make decisions. Get up when the alarm goes off or hit snooze? Make a coffee at home or grab a takeaway? Walk directly towards that stranger in the street or cross over to avoid them? Our brains love shortcuts and avoiding effortful thinking, which keep us stuck in particular grooves.

When it comes to stuff that matters, we want to apply slow and deliberate thinking. When we do so, we are more considered and less likely to react like a jerk. And that's where self-mastery comes in. We use slow thinking when we deliberately lean on specific strengths and put others aside. At first, that will take more effort and consideration. Over time and with practice, we can build the habit of switching between fast thinking (autopilot) and slow thinking (deliberate application). Let's look at the different ways to stay powered up when it comes to relationships.

Building new connections

There is nothing quite like the zing of a new relationship. You may have found a new best friend to hang out with or felt those butterflies of a potential romance. Either way, we experience a pull, a need to spend time with this person and a strong desire to know them. We ask a stack of questions because we feel drawn into their world. We want to be a part of it.

What happens if we need more confidence in making new connections? Or you are connecting with many people but need help finding people with whom you can sustain a connection. Your strengths can be the propellor on your speedboat or the fuel in your Batmobile.

What you expect is how you'll connect.

In Part One, I encouraged you to get to know your iceberg to help you understand and manage your thoughts, feelings and behaviour. I also want you to think about your expectations regarding relationships. You will likely expect different things from different relationships. When you know your expectations, you can test them, adjust them or even step away from them.

For example, we often have particular expectations of people in our inner circle, such as our parents, siblings, partners, children, or pets. When those expectations are unmet, we can feel especially bruised. These relationships should be supportive and warm. They should lift us up and hold us when life gets tough. They should be there through thick and thin.

You will notice there were a lot of 'shoulds' in those statements. We are fed so many messages through the media and, more recently, social media (where everyone seems to be living their best life) about how relationships 'should' be. Yet we know this is not reality.

When we adopt a strengths approach, we appreciate people for who they are. I started this book talking about how many of us feel we are not enough, just as we are. You know by now that when we recognise and appreciate our strengths, we can experience that sense of confidence and ease with who we truly are. We can give that same gift to others by accepting them for their strengths.

That often means putting aside irritation and swapping it for empathy and curiosity. Others' strengths will differ, meaning they see the world differently. Alternatively, we see our strengths reflected back at us, which can also create friction. (More on this soon.)

Let's replace 'that person should behave in this way or that' with 'I can see a real strength in this person'. The more we do this, the more strengths we will see.

Your Back Pocket Coach

Understand your strengths bias. How do your strengths influence the questions you ask? For example, if your strengths allow you to be highly analytical, do you ask about facts rather than feelings?

How are you filtering information based on your strengths?
Do you find some things a turnoff because of a difference in strengths?

How does overusing your strengths impact your relationships?

Building and keeping trust

Humans are hard-wired to connect. Gaining social acceptance is critical for most people, which explains the popularity of social media platforms where we collect likes for the pictures and stories we share. Conversely, our 'not good enough' mentality can get in the way of trusting others.

Strong connections rely on the continued building and keeping of trust. Based on my experience working with individuals, teams and organisations for over 25 years, I have observed three key components that drive trust.

Authenticity: Be yourself. It will help you remain consistent so people know what to expect from you, and you are less likely to be reactive.

Honesty: Set healthy boundaries, ask for what you need, and learn to be assertive to prevent misunderstandings and people-pleasing.

Presence: Give your full attention to the person you are with. Use mindfulness to stay in the moment and prevent fatigue, mistakes and missteps. That does not mean you have to agree with everything others think and say; it means you can have meaningful conversations about what is important to you because you are giving your full attention.

Strengthening connections

Picture this: Your partner/child/friend/colleague comes bounding up and says, 'I've just had the best news!' How you respond will shape that interaction. Depending on your mood, energy levels, and frame of mind, you might offer equal enthusiasm, 'Oh my goodness! Tell me!'. Or, at the other end of the energy spectrum, you might sigh and manage a lukewarm 'Oh yeah...what is it?'.

What type of responder are you – especially when someone shares their good news? According to Shelly Gable and her fellow researchers, there are four distinct styles of responding.[3]

- active constructive: authentic, enthusiastic support

- passive constructive: understated support

- passive destructive: ignoring the event

- active destructive: pointing out negative aspects of the event.

It turns out that how we respond to someone else's good news impacts the relationship. We can strengthen or damage connections. It takes effort to keep relationships strong by staying actively engaged.

In his book *Flourish*, Martin Seligman talks about how he and others worked with current and past members of the US military to address post-traumatic stress disorder (PTSD) through their Master Resilience Program.[4] Seligman and his team applied positive psychology tools, including the deliberate application of strengths, to support recovery and build future resilience.

Much of the program's work focused on helping participants maintain strong, positive relationships with their partners and families. Participants were given tools to reflect on how they could use their strengths to stay active and constructive by being curious and responding enthusiastically and to practice doing so. The results showed a significant positive and lasting improvement in personal relationships.

Here is what those four responding styles look like in practice. Imagine someone close to you has just shared that they just got a job offer.

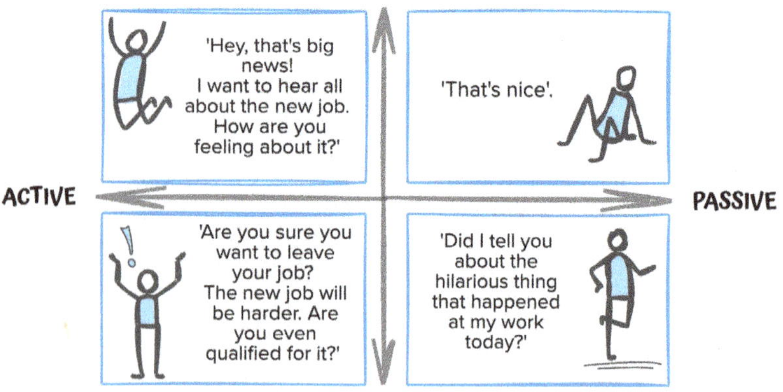

Consider how relationships might transform if we all built habits of active, constructive responding.

Do you remember the last conversation you had with someone close to you? What type of responder were you? How did that impact the conversation if you weren't active/constructive? How might it have been different if you had responded differently?

So many things can prevent us from being fully present and responsive, even (and especially) to those we care about. We might be tired or distracted, or their good news might poke hot buttons for us. Someone else's good news can spark many emotions, including fear, resentment and jealousy. How we choose to respond in the moment will determine whether we build or break trust.

Consider instead which of your strengths put you in a curious frame of mind. Which ones help you stay present and engaged? When you are fully powered up, you will use those self-mastery skills where you use the right strength at the right time and with the right intensity to show up fully for the person sharing their good news. Trust builds when we show the other person, 'I am here for you, right now'.

Swapping speedbumps for launch pads

When you appreciate the strengths of your partner or any other significant person, using your strengths goggles can help smooth out relationship speedbumps. Instead of experiencing a bumpy path, strengths can be a launching ramp for excitement and new experiences.

> 'One of my strengths is my love of learning; I will do that anywhere. I want to know about the place if I'm travelling somewhere. What's the culture and the history? I can't just look at things; I have to learn while there. My Aha moment was learning that I overuse that and drive my husband wild because he doesn't have that same need. He says, "You know, not everything has to be a learning situation". That doesn't mean he's lacking in any way. We have different strengths, and they can complement each other. One of his strengths is bravery. He'll have a go with things that I wouldn't, and he takes me along for the ride. Because of his bravery, I get swept up in experiences that I wouldn't have had if I hadn't been with him.'
>
> – Sandra Wood.

I love Sandra's example. So often, we see difference as a barrier or a speed bump. Imagine how bland life would be if we all enjoyed the same things or saw life similarly. Think of a time when you were invited (or dragged) into a new experience you wouldn't have chosen yet ended up enjoying.

This same approach applies to the mundane elements of everyday life. If you live with other people, everyone has preferences for what they do and don't like to do. And yet, all the stuff around the house needs to be done. When we play to our strengths, we can divide those tasks according to what comes naturally to people. That makes the mundane more palatable.

When we take on tasks that align with our strengths, we catch that wave of energy and pull others along with us. Sandra and her husband Cameron do this when they travel. They ride the waves together and benefit from the energy that each brings, allowing them to turn speedbumps into launch pads.

When the going gets tough, the smart use strengths

When it comes to human interactions, we all likely face conflict. It can come out of the blue like a lightning bolt or brew like a thunderstorm. When we experience conflict, we usually feel a surge of energy as our fight or flight response kicks in. It is our amygdala kicking in and telling us we are in danger. Unfortunately, when our amygdala kicks in, our logical brain (the prefrontal cortex where we do all our considered thinking) taps out.

In most conflict situations, we want to de-escalate and reach a mutual understanding of how to move forward. When we do this successfully, we maintain and even build trust and strengthen the connection.

So, how can we leverage strengths to help us out? The first thing is to engage our prefrontal cortex by asking a curious question.

When a conflict is brewing, or you find yourself in the middle of an unexpected storm, try these questions to fire up the critical thinking part of your brain.

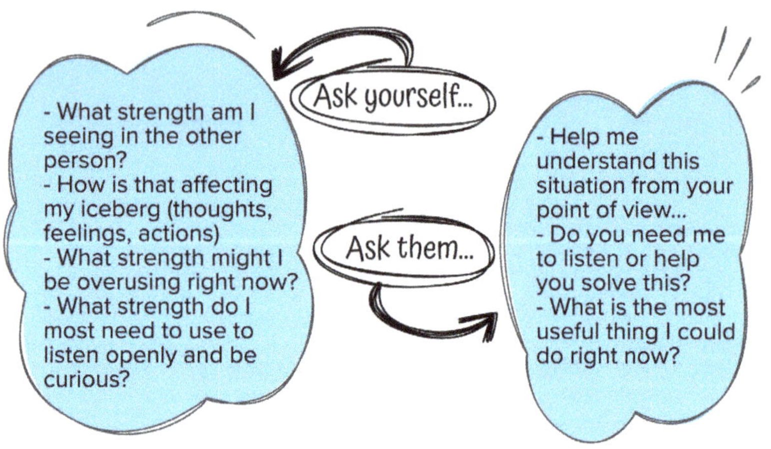

Mirror, mirror

One recent evening, I sat at one end of the lounge reading a book, and my son Ryan sat at the other, laughing at something he was watching on his phone. I looked up and asked, 'What's funny?'. Ryan launched into an explanation about the online clip he was watching. It involved a complicated backstory about a game developer and a whole lot of detail I had no clue about. After about a minute, my face started to twitch with annoyance. Another minute later, he asked bluntly (but not at all rudely), 'You're not really interested in my answer, are you?' I started to protest and make an excuse, mumbled something about being tired, and we returned to our separate, silent tasks.

Later, I reflected on the conversation and realised I'd been a lousy listener. I was irritated by Ryan's long backstory, filled with what seemed to be unnecessary detail. And then it hit me: I do the same thing to others. They ask me a question, and I give them the *whole* story, with all the details. Ryan was holding up a mirror to one of my strengths that I regularly overuse. It was an uncomfortable realisation.

I also recognised that when I experience this irritation in a work context, I work hard to put on my strengths goggles and practice patience. I want to relax at home, so I let my irritation show. Those closest to me get the least disciplined version of me when it comes to managing my strengths.

The next morning, Ryan and I walked to a local café and I shared my 'mirror, mirror' insight with him. We laughed. As we share communication as a strength, we are both aware of our tendency to tell exceptionally long stories.

The message here is that if you find yourself irritated by someone, take a moment to consider whether you are standing in front of a mirror. Is this other person overusing a strength that is the same or similar to yours? Are you on the receiving end of your own behaviour? And while we all want to be able to relax at home and let our strengths flop out (like undoing the zip on your jeans after a big meal), we also want to take care of our relationships. Try a moment of reflection (is that me in the mirror?) and a bit of correction (swap irritation for curiosity). It might avoid putting a dent in your relationship that you later have to panel-beat out with apologies and repairs.

Let's consider how you can use your strengths mindfully and deliberately to take your connections from Warming Up to Powered Up.

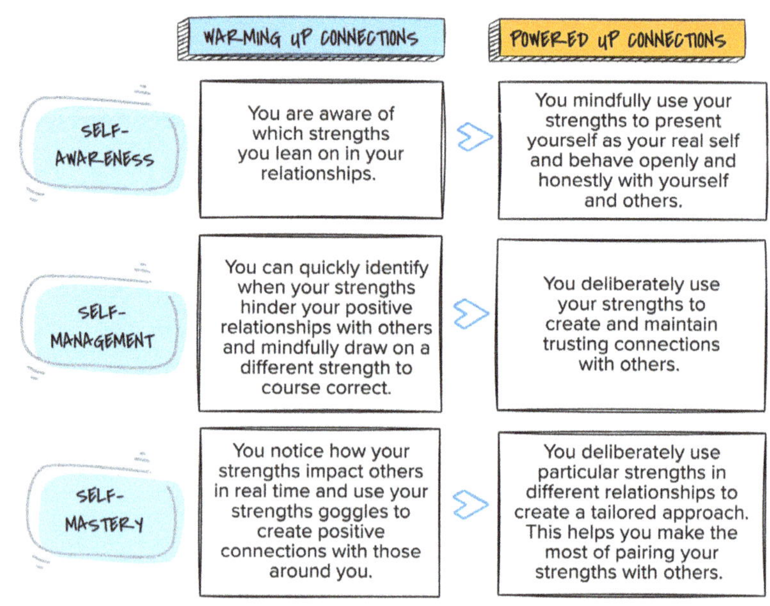

Your Back Pocket Coach

How do you use your strengths to make meaningful connections?
How do you use your strengths when you meet new people? Is it different when you have known someone for a while?

What do you wish your friends and family knew about your strengths?
How do you show that you value and care for others?

When are your strengths misused or overused in your personal relationships? What effect might that have on those relationships?

POWERED UP THRIVING

Learning with strengths

Lifelong learning and strengths

Let's start this chapter by discussing the bigger picture of applying strengths to learning. As a coach, I work with students of every age, from school age to vocational and higher education and in workplaces. Whatever the context, I encourage people to consider powering up their learning by applying their strengths.

I am naturally a learner – it is one of my strengths. For me, learning is like breathing. It is a standing joke in my family that any challenge or misstep in life is just another learning opportunity. 'What can you learn from this?' is a question my sons have long expected when things do not go as planned. I enjoy formal learning and have spent many years studying. I also enjoy learning on the job or just incidentally through life. I have been to weekend workshops to learn pottery, watercolour painting and jewellery making, and I am a Duolingo subscriber to improve my German language skills.

I also apply this strength to my work as a coach and facilitator. If you have this strength, you will likely enjoy helping others learn. You don't need to have the Learner® strength to love learning and take advantage of learning opportunities. Other strengths such as curiosity and perseverance will serve you well.

You might be tackling formal learning or want to improve your ability to learn new information at work or elsewhere. Apply your strengths to the task, and you will dial up your chances of success. In addition to leveraging your strengths, there are other tweaks you can make.

Let's apply the Powered Up model to learning. You can Warm Up with some basic principles, then really fire up your learning by reflecting on the Powered Up questions.

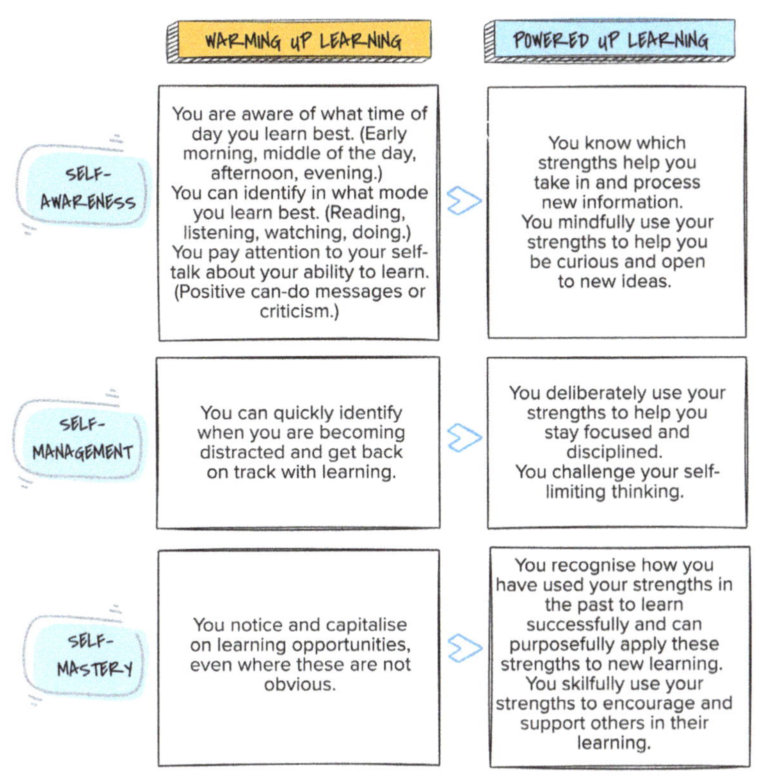

Striving with strengths

Setting and achieving goals

What creates stickiness with achieving goals? It is normal to set a goal and be fired up with enthusiasm and motivation. Over time, other factors kick in, and achieving it becomes more challenging. We get busy, question our priorities, or set other goals that compete for our time and energy.

You can increase your chances of success by setting goals that are aligned with your strengths. You are far more likely to achieve something that feels easier or comes more naturally.

One terrific way to do this is to look at all the goals you have set for yourself. They may be big life goals and smaller short-term goals. Now, look at your strengths. How do these inform your goals? In other words, how do your strengths motivate or guide you to achieve these goals?

My strengths show up most obviously in my big life goals. I have spent most of my adult life engaged in some kind of formal learning. My studies always connect with a long-term personal or professional goal, which speaks to both my Learner® and Futuristic® strengths.

A second way is when you set a goal, consider which of your strengths can be applied deliberately for maximum stickiness. I like to think of this as running through my strengths inventory. It's especially useful when achieving something outside my strengths zone. For example, my work sometimes involves collecting and analysing data. I love the research and collection process, especially when it involves running focus groups or interviews. However, as mentioned earlier, when it comes to sitting down and going through the data, I find it hard to summon much excitement. The work still needs to be done, though, and I can choose my approach.

Without a strengths lens, I dread the task. I procrastinate and find other things to do until the deadline is unavoidable, and then I feel stressed.

When I do a strengths inventory, I know that my energy shifts if I apply my Strategic® strength to data analysis. Instead of dreading the task, I am motivated by the bigger-picture outcomes. What will I uncover by going through the data? What trends and possibilities will I see? The other big-picture element is that I am self-employed, and getting work done efficiently makes good business sense. This approach creates stickiness in terms of achieving the goal. I am far more likely to complete the data analysis when applying my strategic lens.

Hurdle barriers to goal achievement

Let's look at leveraging strengths to overcome hurdles when achieving goals. Imagine your goals are the finish line at the end of a racetrack. Sometimes, you will apply consistent effort (jogging or running) between your current situation and achieving the goal. There will be hurdles along the way where you'll need to motivate yourself and find some explosive energy if you want to succeed. This is where your strengths as superpowers really come into their own.

Procrastination

Recognise procrastination (doing chores, social media scrolling...). Ask yourself 'Why am I avoiding the task?'. What is one thing you could do towards achieving the goal you've set? Lever a strength that helps you do that one thing. Once you start it's likely you'll keep working on it. Reward yourself when you've completed that step.

Overwhelm

You might have set too many goals, the wrong goals, or goals that are not aligned with your strengths. Go back to your iceberg. What are your thoughts and feelings about the goal you are tackling? How are they impacting your behaviour? Which strength could you use to get a different point of view and shift your thinking?

Self doubt

Even the most confident person will have moments of doubt. Which of your strengths do you feel most certain of? Think of a specific time when you used one or more of these strengths and got a boost of confidence. How could you apply a strength in this way right now?

Fear of failure

Sometimes our inner critic tells us we won't succeed and fear of failure causes us to get stuck or spin in circles. Fear makes us blow things out of proportion. When this happens, a great question to ask is 'What is the worst that could happen if I don't achieve this goal?'. Most often, the reality is far less scary than we imagine. Putting things into perspective can help us move from inertia to action.

Negative thinking

Thinking or saying things like 'I'll never be good at this', 'I should be able to do this', or 'I'm so stupid' is a negative thinking trap and self-sabotaging. When did you recently overcome something hard? Which strengths did you use? What result did you get? How you could apply those strengths to your current goal? What would success look like? What's one thing you could do to get closer to achieving that goal?

Choosing a new direction

Life presents us with many crossroads where we can keep going as we are or take a different path. Steve was considering his career options when he took the CliftonStrengths® assessment, which gave him a different perspective.

> 'When I discovered my strengths, I knew I could say, "I can change my career with these strengths. I don't need to be an employee; I can work as a consultant. Give me a situation where it's a mess, and ask me to find the right people, bring them to a team and then get stuff happening. I'm going to love that".'
>
> – Steve Klaassen.

As a coach, I work with people who have reached a crossroads in their personal lives, careers, or both. Choosing a new direction can feel overwhelming and scary. Human brains don't love change, and our instincts tell us to keep the status quo. Yet, if you are unhappy with the status quo, it is worth some short-term discomfort to get a better long-term result. There are ways to smooth some bumps on the path by deciding what to do next and getting to your destination.

I created a set of tools to help clients get clarity, set goals and set themselves up for goal stickiness. I share a condensed version here.

Here's an example of this in action. A few years ago, I worked with Darlene. At 52, she felt ready for a career change. She found that by linking her strengths and values and envisioning the perfect workday, she could make a clear plan and take focused action.

Following these steps will help you to clarify what is important to you and how best to apply your energy to achieve your goal.

Your Back Pocket Coach

Which of your top five strengths helps you take on and understand new information?
How do you best like to learn? Is it through reading, watching others, listening to podcasts or speakers or doing?

How do your top five strengths support you to set goals? What does this look like in action?
Which of your strengths do you most use to achieve goals?
Which of your strengths could you use more to supercharge goal achievement?

Think of a time when you smashed out a goal and exceeded your or others' expectations.
What factors contributed to that success?
Which of your strengths did you lean on the most?

Overcoming adversity

Research shows that character strengths contribute to the full range of human experiences, influencing and creating positive opportunities, and supporting bounce-back from life setbacks. They do so in three ways: buffering – where we use our strengths to prevent problems, reappraisal – where our strengths help us reflect on and reinterpret challenges; and resilience – where we use our strengths to support our bounce-back from setbacks.[1]

In a challenging situation, imagine your strengths as your personal defibrillator. You can apply your Powered Up strengths to shock yourself from inertia or overwhelm and return to a steady rhythm. Apply those paddles once you recognise the frustration, helplessness or confusion that often comes with adversity. And boom! You will be reminded of the power of your strengths. Once you start using those strengths, you will immediately feel a sense of greater clarity and confidence.

> 'If someone is facing a challenge and asks themselves, "What strength can I draw on right now?", they're more likely to go into that challenging situation confidently. They say, "I know I've got this because I've got something to draw on".'
>
> – Sandra Wood.

A career challenge

When I interviewed Kate Webber, she provided a fitting example of handling adversity by skilfully applying her strengths.

> *'I was made redundant a while ago, which was a real shock. I had put in the effort to build such good relationships in my workplace. I'd executed some important things and achieved excellent results. When I was made redundant, it was bruising to feel dispensable. However, I also have strengths that allowed me to reflect on the fact that there were forces outside my control. It was like watching a chess game replayed and seeing how all the different moving pieces impacted others. That really helped me take the sting out of things and make sense of them. Once I went through that process, it was easier to jump back into feeling confident about my skills and strengths*

to start selling myself to other organisations. There were 27 days between walking out the door and having another job offer.'

Kate's ability to appreciate the past might have allowed her to wallow in unfairness and the what-ifs. By Powering Up her strengths, Kate objectively reflected on what had happened. That shifted her out of inertia and into action, which resulted in her moving to a new job opportunity very quickly.

The ultimate personal test

Christopher Miller is a New Zealand-based consultant, strengths coach, and generally terrific guy. I met Christopher through an online forum for coaches, and, in 2020, sought coaching from him when I was working on my own consulting practice.

In 2021, Christopher had the most challenging year of his life when his wife, Fiona, passed away from brain cancer. During Fiona's illness and after her passing, Christopher wrote his book *The Joy of Finding FISH.*[2]

When considering who I wanted to interview for this book, Christopher immediately came to mind. He is a highly insightful coach and strengths practitioner and has generously shared his personal experiences. I asked how his strengths helped him during such a difficult time.

'Three of my strengths dominated during my deepest grieving period: Connectedness®, Maximizer® and Belief®.

Connectedness® was deeply rooted in the belief that everything happens for a reason, there are no coincidences, there is a much bigger reason for why my wife died, and I just hadn't discovered that reason yet.

Maximizer® has the energy of taking one day at a time and making each day a little bit better. There were days when I wanted to stay in bed and not move, but I had to walk the dog and take the kids to school. Regular life imposed itself. My Maximizer® meant that if I could engage a little more with life each day, then things would get better. Now, sometimes it went up and sometimes it went backwards. But Maximizer® was a helpful lens through which I could look at my life and hope for better.

My strength of Belief® means I have always had clear purpose statements, which are very rooted in my values. My purpose, my values and my identity took a huge hit when Fiona died. That was because one of my previous purpose statements was to be a great dad, a loving husband, and an extraordinary coach. And I fully believed in that purpose statement. What do you do when one-third of that statement is no longer true? How do you redefine your life?

I spent about a year drifting without a purpose. I had a valuable conversation with a friend, a strengths coach, that reframed my purpose. Today, my purpose is to honour Fiona and everything I do, to love and support my sons unconditionally, and bring my *love of strengths and FISH (fulfilment, inspiration, success and happiness) to the world.'*

To read more from Christopher, you can find his blog article *How Strengths Saved My Life* on his website at https://christopher-miller.com/2022/09/how-cliftonstrengths-saved-my-life/

Your Back Pocket Coach

Which of your strengths helped you get through your worst day?

Which three of your strengths support you to be resilient? What do they look like in action?

If someone was going through a rough time, what advice might you give them about applying their strengths to the situation?

How do I Power Up?

Knowing and using your strengths regularly is one part of your wellbeing toolkit. Think of your strengths as hand tools. You can add some power tools from positive psychology to help you power up even more.

Some years ago, I had the great fortune to spend two days at a training course with Clown Doctors.[3] The program was all about introducing humour as medicine in spaces such as aged care and disability services. The science was fascinating; when we have a proper belly laugh, our brains release endorphins (happy chemicals) that impact our bodies for 24 hours.

It was obvious within the first half hour that this would be an experience with a difference. When one of the workshop participants excused themselves and went to the bathroom, the facilitator (one of the Clown Doctor founders) asked us to line up quietly outside the bathroom. When our classmate emerged, we gave them a resounding applause. They were surprised, slightly embarrassed and also highly amused. The feel-good high we experienced got our happy hormones firing and, according to science, kept our brains nurtured until the next day.

The positive psychology movement is focused on thriving and boosting wellbeing instead of assuming ill health is inevitable. Just as you might take extra vitamins if you are feeling run-down, positive psychology offers a prescription for boosting your mojo.

Positive psychologists have suggested several practical tools and strategies to boost our resilience and ability to bounce back. Researchers tested these and found that the seven activities in the following figure boosted happiness and reduced symptoms of depression in a six-month trial group.[4]

We know that building muscle strength requires repeatedly doing exercise. One sweaty session has no lasting benefit. In the same way, most of these activities give you the best outcome if you practice them every day for at least a week.

I practice the gratitude strategy every day. My bedtime ritual includes mentally listing at least three things I am grateful for, including the bed I sleep in. Being thankful for something as simple as a bed and reflecting that not everyone has somewhere warm and safe to sleep is an effective way to put challenges into perspective.

I used a mental gratitude list to shift my mood during a particularly tough time a few years ago. I know that I need a regular dose of nature to flourish. Commuting by train to work in a high-rise office building was not helping me. When my mood was low on these train rides, I made a mental list of things I was grateful for. If I had spoken this list out loud, it would have sounded like a meditative chant: 'I am grateful for my sons. I am grateful for my best friend. I am grateful for my good health. I am grateful for my job where I can use my skills. I am grateful for a roof over my head …'. You get the idea. This gratitude practice always gave me a mood lift.

The science behind gratitude is clear. Expressing gratitude, even in our thoughts, energises us in the short term and can inoculate us against future stress. Gratitude is like a booster shot of vitamins each day. It will lift you further if you are feeling good. If you are depleted, the surge of goodness will get you back on track.

Prevention is better than a flat battery

I drive an electric vehicle and when I press the brake, even gently, the car magically adds a little charge to the battery. Okay, so it is not magic; it is mechanics, but it does help prevent battery drain. When I help coaching clients get the most from their strengths, we always talk about how to prevent energy drain.

Picture this scenario: You are talking with someone but getting no traction. You might go around in circles or feel like you are butting your head against a wall. You have tried loads of strategies and nothing is working. You can feel your energy draining.

Self-mastery allows you to take better care of your energy. Knowing your strengths will enable you to work out not only what gives you energy (using your strengths) but also what the energy suckers are or the things that will knock you around. Try the following micro strategies when you need an energy preserver or quick boost.

The force field – imagine an invisible, impenetrable bubble around you. It might be a shimmering dome or a protective energy shield that you project like Invisible Woman.

The strengths flex - start working your way through your strengths. Apply one strength at a time to the challenge or situation. Notice how your energy feels. When you get an energy hit from applying a strength, do something to deliberately use (flex) that strength.

The side step – you don't have to show up to every fight you're invited to. Imagine yourself stepping aside and allowing a conflict or challenge to bypass you.

The scientist – consider the facts of the situation. What evidence do you have for the options or challenges in front of you. How would you measure success or change in this scenario?

The hot-air balloon – take a high-level view of the situation. Get out of the weeds and the details and consider the big picture.

The photographer – what would a camera see? This is an objective way to see things and get some distance from the emotional heat of the situation.

The wise owl - what advice would you give to someone in your situation? Imagine jumping ahead a week, a month or even a year. What action would you take now with the benefit of hindsight?

Zip your lip - pause for 20 seconds before saying anything. Use that time to consider, 'Am I the best person to take this on? Do I have the time or energy? Could someone else do this instead of me? If I say yes, will I take away an opportunity from someone else?'

Add these strategies to your Powered Up toolbox; they are a fantastic way to use your strengths and find clarity, confidence and progress.

Tune in and tune up your energy

Most people don't wait for their cars to break down before they head to a mechanic. They do preventative maintenance: regularly check the oil, replace the tyres when they are worn, make sure the battery connections aren't caked up with gunk ... that sort of thing.

When taking care of our lives, we want to ensure we look after all the important stuff, not just one aspect. Preventative maintenance in key areas can keep us feeling supercharged – or at least not running on fumes. Here are five domains to get you thinking about what gives you energy and how you use your strengths in different areas of life. Ideally, you want to be getting juice from all five.

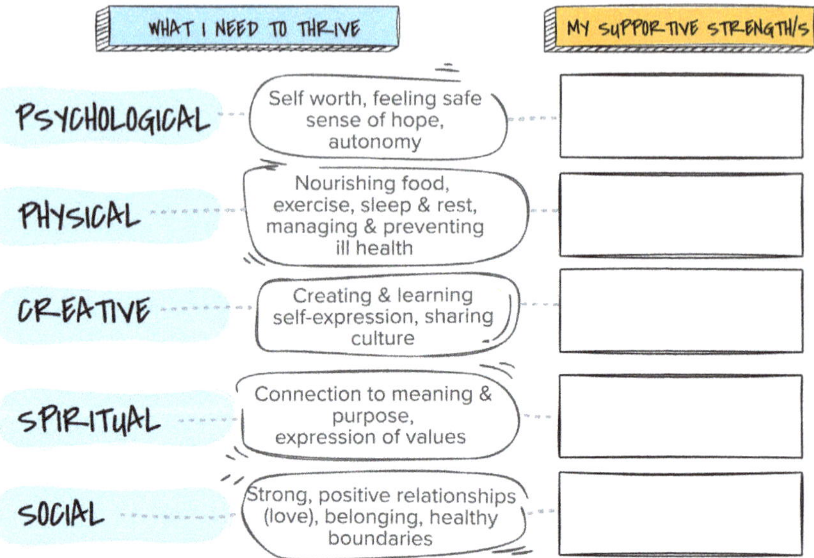

What do you notice when you look at each of the five areas? Are some aspects of your life brimming with energy, while others need a boost? Circle those elements that you feel are well nourished and underline those that need some love.

By working through a mental map like this, you can clearly see what contributes to your thriving and what needs extra attention. You want to achieve balance so you do not rely on one or two domains for your wellbeing. That would be like putting premium fuel in your petrol tank but driving with flat tyres and wondering why you are getting nowhere fast.

Supporting others through adversity

When we see others struggling, it can be tempting to jump into rescuer mode and offer solutions and suggestions. What people mostly need from us is to listen. When we offer a non-judgemental ear, we allow that person the space to clarify their thoughts and feelings and find their own solutions.

We aim to be of service to the other person, not to ourselves. We can put aside our agenda, climb our iceberg, get a view from the top, and be more ears than mouths. One of my favourite strategies is holding space. You can read more about it in an excellent book called *The Art of Holding Space* by Heather Plett.[5] When we hold space for someone, we create a sense of safety by deeply listening and not offering solutions. We are simply with the person as they work through their challenge. We can offer encouragement or support and show them we are not judging them.

In self-mastery mode, we can help others in two ways. The first is to know how to use our strengths to support others. Reflect on how you use your strengths to be a great listener and be present. When we are in listening mode, we can ask curious questions. The coaching questions throughout this book can just as easily be asked of others as used for personal reflection.

We can also help the other person see how they can apply their strengths to the situation. You can help them use the Powered Up model. Here are some tips to get you started.

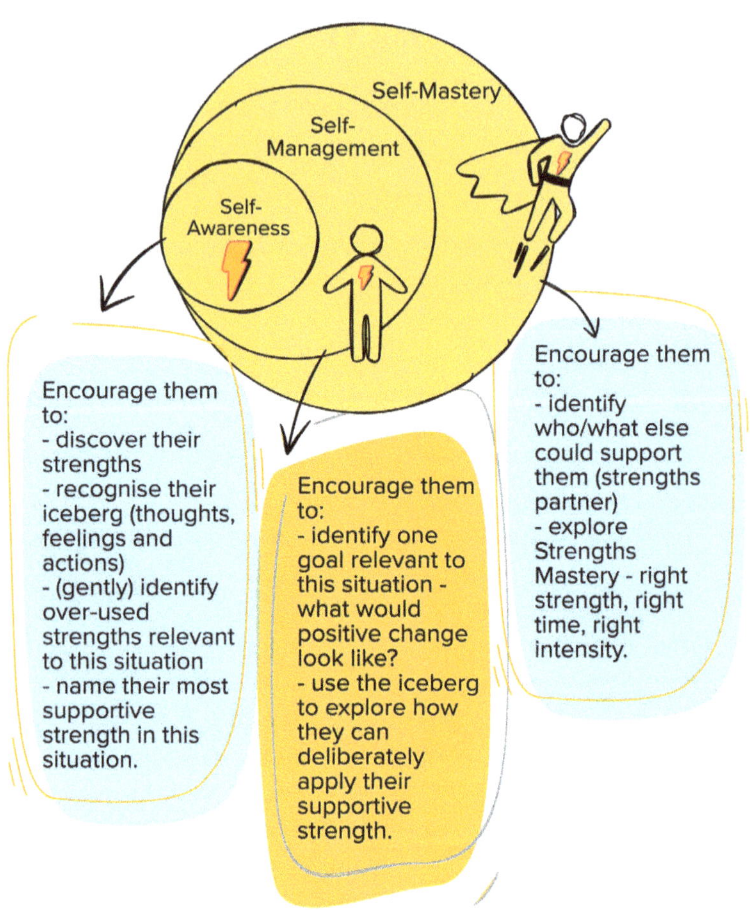

When supporting others in times of adversity, remember to take care of yourself by staying in the strengths mastery zone. Using the right strength at the right time and intensity makes the best possible use of your energy. You are likely to feel energised and in a state of flow. When you know and use your strengths as superpowers, you are at your most resourceful and in the best possible position to support others.

Your Back Pocket Coach

When do you most feel inspired or energised? Which of your strengths are you using when this happens?

Think of a challenge that often comes up for you. What strengths do you admire in others that complement your strengths and could help you tackle this challenge?

What gets in the way of using your strengths? (Hint: it could be fatigue, stress, a sense of time pressure or something else.) Try to think of some specific examples. What was the outcome?

When have you felt energised by helping others in tough situations? Which of your strengths did you lean on to do this?

WHAT'S NEXT

I came late to snow skiing. I started when I was 40, so the natural confidence and ease that come with youth had deserted me. To begin with, I was extremely wobbly and rather clueless. The first thing I did was book a lesson with an instructor who taught me the fundamental skills. I have taken lessons every year since then – usually more than one. I figured out very quickly that if my confidence and skills were going to improve, I needed coaching.

As a result, my skiing has improved exponentially, and I fall over less than I would have if I had struggled alone. Ski coaching gives me more quality time doing something I love and doing it better and better. It helps me develop my skiing superpowers (still intermediate but improving constantly!).

When you first picked up this book, you may have wondered what your superpowers were and if you even had any. Self-doubt might have been a more familiar feeling than 'I've got this!'. I hope you are feeling energised, inspired and empowered with the knowledge that your strengths are your *superpowers*.

The Powered Up model shows you how to work on self-awareness as a starting point. Knowing ourselves and our superpowers is critical foundation work. Once we have done this, we can build self-management. No longer ping-ponging through life, we can chart our course, using our strengths as levers to get the best impact from our energy. Once your self-management strategies are sorted, you can leap to self-mastery. That is where you use your superpowers for good, not evil. Here, you can partner with others, help them know and use their superpowers and create winning combinations.

Now that you have read my book and have new strategies and tools, I hope you have tested some and turned them into habits. I have shown you how to power up your work and relationships and thrive with strengths. The beauty of your superpowers is that they have limitless applications. Use them anywhere and everywhere!

Now that you have had a taste of how to think more deeply about your strengths and apply them, what happens next? I am here to help you get Powered Up. Working with a strengths coach will supercharge your efforts to achieve self-mastery. Coaching is a fast track to suiting up and putting your superpowers to work.

'The power of the strengths tool came from
having a personalised understanding of how to
use it, and coaching was incredibly valuable.
I was walking through a particular challenge
and building the strengths language into
my work. It's the deliberateness I like.'

– Kate Webber.

From the get-go, coaching helps you make sense of your strengths report and apply your strengths to get the best from them. It is about making the most of the information in your strengths report. A good coach can help you unpack the report and understand how the language of strengths applies to you. A great coach will help you find those light-bulb moments of self-discovery where you truly *see* and appreciate who you are. Coaching and self-mastery go hand in hand.

> 'Strengths coaching should be mandatory and something everyone gets to do at some point. It's really powerful to sit down with someone and have your strengths validated and reality checked.'
>
> **– Peggy Webb.**

And finally, quite plainly and possibly most eloquently:

> 'Mentoring and coaching should be part of every work schedule constantly, not as a once-off when things are bad.'
>
> **– Kerry Grace.**

When you are ready to get Powered Up, come and find me! We can work together individually, with your work team or other group, or even to create change in your community. You can reach me in the following ways:

Nicole@nicoleweber.com.au
www.linkedin.com/in/nicoleweberconsultant

TOOLS AND RESOURCES

Strengths list

Adaptable	Focused	Practical
Ambitious	Helpful	Proactive
Articulate	Honest	Prudent
Calm	Humble	Punctual
Candid	Imaginative	Realistic
Capable	Independent	Reflective
Charismatic	Innovative	Reliable
Clear-headed	Insightful	Resilient
Communicative	Intuitive	Resourceful
Competitive	Inventive	Respectful
Considerate	Kind	Responsible
Consistent	Logical	Responsive
Cooperative	Loyal	Self-confident
Courageous	Methodical	Self-disciplined
Creative	Motivated	Sense of humour
Curious	Natural leader	Sensible
Decisive	Objective	Sincere
Dedicated	Open-minded	Sociable
Detail oriented	Optimistic	Strategic thinker
Determined	Organised	Systematic
Diligent	Outspoken	Team player
Efficient	Passionate	Thorough
Emotionally intelligent	Patient	Thoughtful
Empathetic	Perceptive	Trustworthy
Energetic	Persistent	Versatile
Engaging	Personable	Well-rounded
Enthusiastic	Persuasive	Willing
Flexible	Positive	Witty

Iceberg worksheet

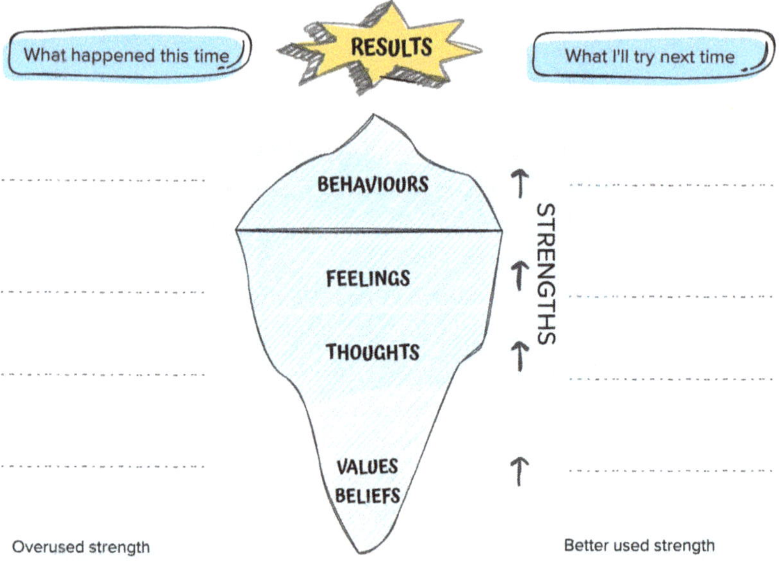

Tune into strengths worksheet

STARS worksheet

FURTHER READING

The following books are excellent strengths-based resources.

Celebrating Strengths: Building Strengths-based Schools by Jennifer M. Fox Eades.

Finding FISH in a Strengths-Based Practice: Fulfilment, Inspiration, Success and Happiness by Christopher Miller.

The Joy of Finding FISH: A Journey of Fulfilment, Inspiration, Success and Happiness by Christopher Miller.

Go Put Your Strengths to Work by Marcus Buckingham.

Strengths Based Parenting: Developing Your Children's Innate Talents by Mary Reckmeyer and Jennifer Robison.

The Brain and Strengths Based School Leadership by Sheryl G. Feinstein and Robert W. Kiner.

The Strengths Approach: Sharing power, building hope, creating change by Wayne McCashen.

The Strengths-Based Organisation: How to boost inclusivity, wellbeing and performance by Emily Hutchinson and Caroline Brown.

The Wiley Blackwell Handbook of the Psychology of Positivity and Strengths-based Approaches at Work by Lindsay G. Oades, Michael F. Steger, Antonella Delle Fave and Jonathan Passmore (Eds).

Working with Children and Adolescents in Residential Care: A strengths-based approach by Bob Bertolino.

Your Child's Strengths: A guide for parents and teachers by Jenifer Fox.

ABOUT THE AUTHOR

Nicole Weber is a consultant and self-confessed strengths super-enthusiast. She appreciates how her strengths have allowed her to build a successful consulting practice based on 30 years of industry experience, whilst readily admitting when they spark overly ambitious five- or ten-year plans.

Nicole is most energised and filled with joy when working with individuals and teams to create personal and cultural transformation, where strengths are discovered and leveraged. She has worked with people from all walks of life across government, non-profit and business sectors. When Nicole isn't working, she usually has some studies, travel plans or a building/renovation project on the go (or all of these at once). She calls the Snowy Mountains home.

www.nicoleweber.com.au

REFERENCES

1. Seligman, M. E. P. & Csikszentmihalyi, M. (2000). Positive Psychology: An Introduction. *The American Psychologist.* 55. 5-14. https://doi.org/10.1037/0003-066X.55.1.5

2. Seligman, M. E. P. (2002). *Authentic happiness: Using the new positive psychology to realize your potential for lasting fulfilment.* New York, NY: Free Press.

3. Csikszentmihalyi, M. (1990). *Flow: the psychology of optimal experience.* New York, NY: Harper and Row.

4. Dolev-Amit, T., Rubin, A. & Zilcha-Mano, S. (2020). Is awareness of strengths intervention sufficient to cultivate wellbeing and other positive outcomes? *Journal of Happiness Studies,* 1-22. https://doi.org/10.1007/s10902-020-00245-5.

5. Peterson, C. & Seligman, M. E. P. (2004). *Character strengths and virtues: A handbook and classification.* New York, NY: Oxford University Press and Washington, DC: American Psychological Association.

6. Hutchinson, E. & Brown, C. (2021). *The strengths-based organization: how to boost inclusivity, wellbeing and performance.* Tadley, England: Practical Inspiration Publishing.

7. Gallup®.com. Available at https://www.Gallup®.com/ CliftonStrengths®/en/253754/history-CliftonStrengths®. aspx#ite-254129.

8. Isen, A.M., Rosenzweig, A.S. and Young, M.J. (1991). The influence of positive affect on clinical problem solving. *Medical Decision*

Making, 11(3), pp.221–227. https://doi.org/10.1177/027298
9x9101100313.

9. Isen, A. M., Daubman, K. A. & Nowicki, G. P. (1987). Positive affect facilitates creative problem solving. *Journal of Personality and Social Psychology*, 52(6), 1122-1131. https://doi.org/10.1037/0022-3514.52.6.1122.

10. Isen, A. M. (2003). Positive affect as a source of human strength. In L.G. Aspinwall & U. M. Staudinger (Eds), A psychology of human strengths: fundamental questions and future directions for a positive psychology (pp. 179-195). *American Psychological Association*. https://doi.org/10.1037/10566-013

11. Estrada, C. A., Isen, A. M. & Young, M. J. (1997). Positive affect facilitates integration of information and decreases anchoring in reasoning among physicians. *Organizational Behavior and Human Decision Processes*, 72(1), 117. https://doi.org/10.1006/obhd.1997.2734.

12. Csikszentmihalyi, M. (1990). *Flow: The psychology of optimal experience*. Harper Perennial: New York.

13. Seligman, M. E. P. & Csikszentmihalyi, M. (2000). Positive Psychology: An introduction. *American Psychologist, 55*(1), 5-14. https://doi.org/10.1037/0003-066X.55.1.5

14. Buckingham, M. & Clifton, D. (2001). *Now, discover your strengths: how to develop your talents and those of the people you manage.* New York, NY: Gallup Press.

15. Peterson, C. & Seligman, M. E. P. (2004). *Character strengths and virtues: A handbook and classification.* New York, NY: Oxford University Press and Washington, DC: American Psychological Association.

16. Sorenson, S. (2014). How employees' strengths make your company stronger. [online] Gallup.com. Available at: https://www.gallup.com/workplace/231605/employees-strengths-company-stronger.aspx.

17. Buckingham, M. (2010). *Go put your strengths to work: 6 powerful steps to achieve outstanding performance.* New York, NY: Free Press.

18. Hall, E. T. (1976). *Beyond culture.* New York, NY: Anchor Books.

19. Gallup®.com. Employee Engagement. https://www.gallup.com/394373/indicator-employee-engagement.aspx. (Accessed 25/6/2024.)

20. Seligman, M.E.P. (2011). *Flourish: A new understanding of happiness and well-being and how to achieve them.* London: Nicholas Brealey Publishing.

21. Covey, S. R. (1989). *The 7 habits of highly effective people: restoring the character ethic.* New York: Simon & Schuster.

22. www.abc.net.au. (2017). *General David Morrison's torrid 12 months.* [online] Available at: https://www.abc.net.au/news/2017-01-25/australian-of-the-year-general-david-morrisons-torrid-12-months/8212248.

23. Hall, V. (2007). *The simple truth about trust.* Sydney, NSW. Entente.

24. Waldinger, R. & Schulz, M. (2023). *The Good Life: Lessons from the World's Longest Scientific Study of Happiness.* New York, NY: Simon & Schuster

25. Kahnemann, D. (2007). *Thinking, Fast and Slow.* New York, NY: Farrar, Straus and Giroux.

26. Gable, S.L., Reis, H.T., Impett, E.A. & Asher, E.R. (2004). What Do You Do When Things Go Right? The Intrapersonal and Interpersonal Benefits of Sharing Positive Events. *Journal of Personality and Social Psychology*, 87(2), pp.228–245. doi:https://doi.org/10.1037/0022-3514.87.2.228.

27. Seligman, M.E.P. (2011). *Flourish: A new understanding of happiness and well-being and how to achieve them.* London: Nicholas Brealey Publishing.

28. Niemiec, R. (2019). Six Functions of Character Strengths for Thriving at Times of Adversity and Opportunity: a Theoretical Perspective. *Applied Research in Quality of Life*, 15, 551-572. https://doi.org/10.1007/S11482-018-9692-2.

29. Miller, C. (2022). *The Joy of Finding FISH*, Hambone Publishing.

30. Clown Doctors. https://humourfoundation.org.au/clown-doctors/

31. Gander, F., Proyer, R.T., Ruch, W. & Wyss, T. (2012). Strength-based positive interventions: Further evidence for their potential in enhancing well-being and alleviating depression. *Journal of Happiness Studies*, [online] 14(4), pp.1241–1259. https://doi.org/10.1007/s10902-012-9380-0.

32. Plett, H. (2021). *The Art of Holding Space: A Practice of Love, Liberation, and Leadership*. Page Two.